About the Author

Michael C Richards was born in a modest two-bedroom council flat in Cardiff, South Wales. He is married to Patricia and has two grown up children; Lee and Rhian. He started his working life in the infamous Tiger Bay and he quickly learnt the meaning of the word survival.

Happy Christmas
2016
Love Sharon.
X

Dedication

The book is dedicated to my wife and children; without them my soul would not have survived.

Thanks to HSBC, Cega Air, and the incredible staff at Hospital De Levant in Porto Cristo.

Michael C Richards

HALLUCINATIONS OR REALITY

AUSTIN MACAULEY
PUBLISHERS LTD.

A CIP catalogue record for this title is available from the British Library.

ISBN 9781786121523 (Paperback)
ISBN 9781786121530 (Hardback)
ISBN 9781786121547 (E-Book)

www.austinmacauley.com

First Published (2016)
Austin Macauley Publishers Ltd
25 Canada Square
Canary Wharf
London
E14 5LQ

Acknowledgments

This book would never have been written without some help from some amazing people. Doctor Sospedra and his incredible team at the Hospital De Llevant in Porto Cristo, Mallorca, a heartfelt thank you.

The gentleman at HSBC Travel Insurance help line who was so wonderful and helpful to my wife in her moment of absolute terror. My friend, I wish I could meet you and one-day hope that I do track you down.

Our friends and close family who supported Pat while all hell was breaking loose, you all know who you are, a big thank you.

The main reason I wrote this book was to honour my family, as I said early on without them my soul would have died, they kept me going. Lee, Rhian, Daley, Tracey, Ayla, Lola, Caleb, Dexter and Koen. You know I love you all.

On a technical side, thank you to Erica for her proof reading and technical skills on my computer and to Neil at Brightcall for being there when the IT side has proved a challenge.

My last acknowledgement is to Leo McCrindle, it may sound a minor role, but it was quite a major one in my mind, thank you for taking such good care of my pigs.

In The Beginning

I had known about the presence for a long time, since early childhood, it was only really explained to me at the age of eleven, I say explained; that sounds very simplistic, I came to terms with it at the age of eleven.

The presence certainly saved my life on one occasion and was there for me during my teenage years at moments of fear and hostility, she said farewell as I married and I had not seen her again until my period of madness.

Again, madness is a very easy and simple word to bolt various incidents together and provide an explanation for the unexplained.

I hope that through this book, I have given an insight into what I think the word madness really covers, but I don't think I have done it justice enough.

The rabbit was my first pet, she had two babies, one was dead at birth, the irony of this will be seen as the book progresses and how life changes from idyllic to sheer terror.

That life still continues is a miracle in itself, madness in fact.

Hallucinations or Reality

This book is a true story of events that took place in Mallorca, September 2014. *Hallucinations or Reality* that is for you the reader to decide, however we would say that every detail is factual and at the time very scary.

We would like to thank numerous people who helped us when we most needed them:

Dr Sospedra and his team at the Hospital De Llevant; their care was incredible. They saved Mike's life.

The staff at the Royal Berkshire Hospital in the UK, again their care was second to none.

The crew at Cega who re-patriated Mike and looked after him so well during the flight.

And finally, to HSBC who handled all the arrangements for the medical cover, their support was so much appreciated at a time that is hard to describe.

We would both like to say no thanks go to a strangulated hernia, septicaemia and double pneumonia, they are all killers, look after your body.

Casa Bora

Nothing unusual about Casa Bora, three bed detached villa overlooking the harbour at Cala d'Or, not in the greatest spot, the ring road went past the villa and could be quite busy in the morning and early evening, but for a perfect sun trap it was hard to beat and the pool made sure you never got over heated. We had bought the villa about three years ago and had been out there every month for the last two of those years. Sometimes for a week but mostly for two.

We had become friends with most of the local shop owners and there was always a drink on our table at our local bar before we sat down, our Spanish still clumsy was gradually improving although we both struggled with the local garden centre, but with Pidgin English and Spanish and a lot of pointing we managed to get by. Some plants didn't turn out the way we thought they would but this was part of the fun.

Our kids and grandchildren certainly had some fun times in Casa Bora and loved going down to the nearby beaches, four in total and each one unique. One common denominator was the beach peddler who used all four beaches to peddle his wares. The grandchildren were always first in line when he cut up coconuts, mangos and pineapples in front of them and offered them a little taster to entice the gullible grandparents into forking out the cash for the real thing. The grandkids were so impressed with the beach man that they used to talk about him in their sleep, their first Spanish words were 'Coc, Banana, Pineapple, Melo, Oeoe'.

Life at Casa Bora was ideal but how that was going to change over the next six months was unbelievable.

We are Mike and Pat Richards, a middle aged couple, although if you believe the papers we are all going to live to 120 in the next decade, so we could be described as young but that would be just fooling ourselves and would mess up the stats for the national papers.

Married with two grown children who have families of their own, and have given us five grandchildren, three dogs, two pigs and a couple of chickens that seem to like to attack us whenever they see us.

We live in Wargrave, Berkshire and moved up from Cardiff thirty-four years ago when my job went down to a three-day week and I had to look for an alternative career as we were just starting a family.

Pat's cousin lived in Twyford so we originally settled there and remained in Twyford, although moving around the village in three different houses, for twenty-eight years.

It was when we sold our company in 2008 that we decided to look for a place in Mallorca; it took us nearly two years to find our ideal place named Casa Bora. Location was very important; we didn't want to spend half the time behind the wheel of a car when we were over there. The villa was fully furnished so it was a case of meeting on a Friday morning in Palma, signing no end of documents, shaking hands with everyone around the table at least twice and then moving in that afternoon, very happy days.

Now we need to start on our real life drama, scary it might be but it happened, explanations, well that's up to you the reader.

Chapter 1

The First Touch; how it all began

Saturday night and in traditional Spanish style, Pat is watching *Strictly*, and then *X Factor*, nothing changes no matter where you are in the world. I'm outside on the patio, catching the last rays and BBQing some monster chicken breasts. The Mallorcan butchers are second to none with the sizes of their meat. The chicken breasts look more like a side of pork, never mind a good excuse to chuck another San Miguel down the throat while making sure that the meat is cooked thoroughly. Lee and Tracey had gone out for a last night's meal and the grandkids were safely tucked up in bed, peace reigned.

Timed to perfection *X Factor* has just finished, and to our surprise the uncle of a friend of ours got through to the next stage, a cheap glass of Freixenet to celebrate.

Right, chicken torn to pieces, jacket potato no longer exists, time for feet up and watch the next part of *Breaking Bad*. The villa had two sofas, both with patio doors behind them so it was not only comfortable to veg out but you also had a nice breeze to keep you chilled. My sofa was nothing special, seen action by man and animals by the look of the scratches on the one arm, we knew the previous owner had a cat, we spent a lot of time on cleaning and air freshener to get rid of the smell, never quite sure we achieved our goal.

It all started so innocently, just came to an interesting and violent part of the DVD when I felt a poke in the back, nothing painful but just enough to make you think, what was that. Pat annoyed because I freeze framed the DVD but I wanted to check behind sofa to make sure no cat had crept in with the patio doors open. There was nothing to be seen, no mark on sofa, nothing around so I just ignored it. Tried to explain it to myself but the only explanation was that a rogue spring had speared me. Curiosity satisfied we watched the end of the DVD, closed up the doors and went to bed. I must admit I did look behind the sofa just once more, looking for that rogue spring. Incident forgotten and life went on as normal.

The land behind and to the side was mainly to shrub but with a few little patches where prickly pears were growing, the grandchildren loved going in there and watching me attempt to pick some pears while singing the famous couple of lines from the *Jungle Book*, a few sore fingers but hey they were happy. We stumbled on a stray cat who had just had about five kittens, couldn't quite see them all, but mum was not happy that we were there. Gathered up the kids and made a quick exit.

The next day we drove everyone to the airport, September was fast approaching and the first taste of school was beckoning for the two four year olds. The conversation in the back of the car was interesting from the two of them, they couldn't wait till show and tell, to tell their class about the prickly pears and the lion they came across, at least no lack of imagination there.

The usual sad goodbyes, loads of kisses and roll on half term and Christmas, although we were not to know our visit to the UK for half term was not going to take place.

Chapter 2

Come October and the resort of Cala D'Or no longer exists, there are still some bars and the local Spar open in the village with the big supermarket, Eroski, staying open all year round. The weather is quite good in October, a few rainy days but usually comfortable enough to sit outside for a coffee or a glass of wine should the mood take you.

The strangest thing is the total lack of people, the streets are empty, the beaches look superb with the sun shining down on them but not a person to be seen. It's just like a ghost town, and any moment you expect a bale of hay and some tumble weed to come rolling down the road. I do walk down to the Spar each day and pick up my paper and a beautiful French stick, piping hot, Pat thinks the old woman has a soft spot for me, because she cooks the bread as I arrive and then makes me a cup of coffee while I wait. She shocked me the first day she did this, I sat down at the counter and in my best Spanish said, 'Gracias,' the next moment she is talking to me in fluent English albeit in a heavy Spanish accent. I asked her why she never spoke English during the summer and she said why should I, no one speaks Spanish to me. This routine went on most days during the off season, a 15-minute chat while the bread cooked and the coffee was drunk, she even knew the football scores and turned out she was a big fan of Chelsea, she loved the chosen one.

The one thing that does stay open all year round is Burger King, always useful if there is a power cut at the villa. On one such Saturday night I grabbed a torch and ventured down to the village hoping that Burger King's generator was working. Big surprise, it was working and there was a children's party in there. Now unfortunately fast food they are not, if I ask for two different items with different sides it takes about three of them to sort it out and then I have to check it, the number of times I have got back to the villa with either the fries missing or onion rings gone astray. With twenty kids to be served, I placed my order, grabbed a beer in a plastic cup, a perk of Spanish fast food outlets, and sat down at a table and waited. Chaos reigned, there was a procession of parents picking up their kids' food and then coming back to the counter for the missing items. I was just about to grab another beer when they called my order. Happy days, now to leg it back to the villa before it got cold, thank God for the torch.

To my surprise when I got home, Pat had lit all the candles around the patio, so we had a very romantic Burger King meal under the moonlight. We were joined by some friends, the cat, aka lion, and her kittens walked across the patio without a care in the world, only sad thing; there were only 4 kittens, one obviously didn't make it.

Meal eaten, candles put out and magically the electric came back on so we settled down to the last series of *Breaking Bad*. Twenty minutes in and I felt something rubbing against my back through the sofa, 'That bloody cat's in here!' I shouted, jumped up and looked behind the sofa, nothing, five mins of pushing the sofa, taking the cushions off but no sign of the cat.

Pat, pretty exasperated, said, 'How much did you have to drink when you were out? Let me sit there and you have my sofa.' Within minutes I felt a sharp dig in my back, again I reacted badly, searching like a headless chicken for the suspected cat, I found nothing. Pat said, 'This is bloody stupid, I'll sit on the sofa with you,' no more contact. 'Well at least we know it's scared of me,' Pat said sarcastically.

We went to bed both agreeing that *Breaking Bad* was pretty awesome, that was in between Pat taking the piss about things that went bump in the night.

The next day Pat was having a bath and for some unknown reason I wanted to go and see the cat and kittens, I climbed through the shrubs and came to where we had found them last time.

I threw up in horror, spitting phlegm everywhere, there in front of me were the cat and kittens all beheaded and lying in a circle.

Chapter 3

After the initial shock, I tried to compose myself to go back to the villa but I could not get the sight of the cat and kittens out of my head, who could have done such a thing and why. Cala D'Or is not renowned for its yobs and surely they would have had to use a torch which could have been seen by us or a passer-by.

I walked down to the marina when Pat phoned, 'Where are you?'

'I just wanted some fresh air, will be back now,' I sat on the bench for a few minutes just to collect my thoughts; do I tell Pat or just keep it to myself? On the walk back I decided to keep shtum and act if nothing had happened.

The next couple of days were awkward, I kept thinking about the cat, Pat being very attentive worried that I was coming down with something, in fact I did have a very sore throat but put that down to the retching when I saw the cat and kittens in such a state.

I had not been back, although I felt guilty, that I should at least bury them or cover them in some way. Pat was going to have her hair cut that afternoon and as the nearest place open was in Manacor she would be gone for a good hour and a half. I would dig up two buckets of earth and put this over them and if that was not enough another two buckets would do it.

I filled two buckets and crept around the shrubland like a naughty school boy. I got to the cats prepared for the worse, expecting maggots to have been having a field day, but there was nothing except for a little grave with a small cross on top of it. The cross had something written on it, I could not read it without kneeling down. Half expecting something to leap out of the grave I carefully read it and read it again to make sure I was correct, one word both sides of the cross: 'GRACIAS'. I was truly getting spooked; I emptied both the buckets and left rather quicker than I arrived.

On Pat's return I decided to keep all this to myself still and not involve her. I hoped that the mystery was now over and that it could be forgotten, although my mind was like a pin ball machine with so many things going through it.

Two weeks went past, no more sofa incidents, in fact I was becoming quite relaxed and although I still had unanswered questions, I was beginning to relax more. I did want to confide with the old lady down the Spar, but somehow did not know where to start. I thought she might put me down as a crazy Brit who had changed to cider rather than stick to the beer.

We had decided, as it was Friday and the sun was shining, we would have a cultural day in Palma. Start off with the cathedral, it's just like a sun kissed Notre Dame, if not more gothic, find a tapas bar probably La 5a Puneta, we usually start off with pintxos, which are Basque style snacks on cocktail sticks, they are so filling that we usually end with them at the same time as we start. They have a neat way of charging, they just count up the number of sticks with each one equalling about a euro 50 cents, a glass of wine to wash it all down and then a leisurely stroll down to the marina to see what celebrities' yachts are moored up. There's always great excitement when a cruise liner is coming into port, nothing more peaceful than supping a latte as you watch the captain manoeuvre the liner into place.

Feeling totally relaxed we headed home, the only downside was that I felt as if I was coming down with man flu. Feeling a bit groggy by the time we got home, I thought I would have an early night, plus I would sleep in the spare bedroom just to keep my germs away from Pat.

A stiff whisky and I was asleep before I knew it. I woke to a whirling sound, I could just see the alarm clock and it said 2am. The whirling sound was coming from above my head and it sounded as if it was gaining speed, all I could see were two bright green lights just like eyes looking at me.

I found the sideboard light switch and there above my head was a bird on a chain swinging around in circles, it was getting faster and its eyes seemed to be focused on me all the time. My eyes were getting used to the light and I could see that the bird was green and white but made of some sort of metal, tin sprang to mind but cannot be sure of that. My brain was not working fast enough to take this in, the bird suddenly stopped and just hung there staring at me. The next moment I heard a scratching noise, I looked down onto the floor and there was a rabbit, a real life rabbit not made of tin, it looked at me and scurried into the wardrobe.

By this time, I was sweating and scared, was it a fever coming out in me or was I going mad? I then realised that the window was wide open, in my mind I tried to work this out as an explanation but knew it was useless, how did the rabbit jump five feet to get through the window? And did the bird? Where was the bird? It had disappeared. Did the bird get blown in and get itself tangled on the light? Even in my confused state I knew this was bullshit but I pretended it gave me some comfort. The next thing the window slammed shut with such a loud bang that it woke Pat and she came in thinking I had fallen out of bed.

I played dumb and said I was coming down with something nasty, she noticed I was sweating and just tucked me in and went back to her bed, saying she'll call the doctor in the morning and make me an appointment to see him.

Laying there in the dark I had so many thoughts going through my head I could not roll over and get to sleep, I just stared into the dark, wondering what on earth was happening to my mind and body.

Looking into the dark abyss I realised a form was taking shape, the more I stared the more I realised it was the shape of a young girl, she smiled and put her finger to her lips, telling me to be quiet, she was then gone.

I was suddenly calm. I had encountered this form before, albeit the last time was thirty-seven years ago.

Chapter 4

The Meeting

Thirty-seven years ago is a long time but I remember the presence of the form as if it was yesterday. It was the night before our wedding and I was again finding it hard to sleep, the form appeared in the darkness and she blew me a kiss and waved goodbye. Since that date, April 22nd 1977, she has not shown herself, although I have felt her presence on certain occasions.

The form or should I say girl, has never spoken or touched me, she has always remained the same size and looked about five or six years of age. She is a pretty blonde haired girl who oozes psychic powers.

She first appeared when I was fishing on the banks of the river Taff along with my dog, Flash. We were after eels that lived in abundance in the river. Not much you could do with them but it was fun and made a break from playing football with all the other kids in the street. I had caught about eight and had them in my net when a buzzing noise started, it intensified and Flash started crying, then suddenly a wind came up that blew my bait box about thirty feet away. Flash would not move and all I wanted to do was scarper. The buzzing stopped at the same time as the wind, I looked at the electrical pylon nearby and it was sparking with rogue voltage going through it. I had enough, I went to empty the eels back in the river and they were all dead. I grabbed my rod and went to leg it when I first saw the hazy form in front of me. I stood still not knowing what to do and then it disappeared, that was my cue to get the hell out of there. I think that was the first time me and Flash ran all the way home, collapsing outside the front door. My mum was working, so I felt through the letter box and grabbed the key that was on a piece of string and unlocked the door. Inside I realised how much I was shaking, Flash went straight to his bed and did not move all night. When my mum came home from work she thought there was something wrong with him, he didn't even come out of the bed for his tea.

Not a good night's sleep, but next morning I was eager to go back to the river, needed to get my keep net. I was scared, but pure curiosity edged me on. I didn't want to go on my own, not brave enough for that, so I went and knocked for Mike Williams and asked him if he would come and help me untangle my keep net with the dead eels in, he said sure his dog needed a walk anyway. We talked football most of the way, Mike was three years older than me and played football for the school team, he was goalie based on the fact that he was the tallest in the school.

We got down to the gate for the field and Flash started playing up, he was off the lead but would not move any further than the gate, I had to leave him there but then as we approached the keep net Mike's dog also got all spooked and ran back to where Flash was sat. I pulled up the keep net and there inside were about a dozen live eels. Mike, bemused, said, 'I thought you said they were dead?' I looked shocked, I'm sure they were, every one of them.

He then pointed to the other side of the Taff and there were hundreds of dead eels all along the bank. 'Here,' he said, 'let's empty the net and get the hell out of here, I'm feeling spooked like the dogs.' I emptied the net and returned the eels back to the river, they didn't sense freedom for long, they all keeled over and died. Mike had enough, 'Look, there's some real shit going down here, let's get back to the street and tell the rest of the gang.'

That was my first encounter with my friend the young blonde girl but it was not going to be my last I sensed.

We got back to the street and by the time Mike had told our story, albeit blown out of some proportion, not many of us went down the fields fishing for eels for quite some time.

I did not tell him about the appearance of my friend; I thought that might be too much to take.

It was not until a couple of years later that I realised my friend and I were closer than I thought.

Chapter 5

Life Forms

Pat came into the bedroom early, 'How are you feeling?'

'Not bad, at least the temperature has gone down, not sweating so much now, will get up shortly and see how I feel.'

'Let me make you an appointment with the doctor, you looked terrible last night.'

'Let me get up and I will decide; I'm going for a shower.'

It was a beautiful morning and the last thing I wanted to do was spend the morning at the doctors, where I will probably end up with a bottle of antibiotics but in all honesty, I was still feeling strange.

Yes, I did end up at the doctors, yes I did have a bottle of antibiotics and a little surprise four blood tests. Even in a heavy Spanish accent, it still raised a smile to my face, 'Senor you will feel a little prick,' hey ho, simple things please simple minds.

Back home to a little bit of sun bathing, Pat already out there making the most of it, 'What about a walk to the marina?'

'OK,' I said. 'But not too late, still feeling a bit groggy through lack of sleep. Not sure what will be open but we can take a look.'

We found La Bodega open so had a plateful of tapas with a couple of glasses of house white. On the way home Pat asked how I felt. I said, 'Fine but tired.'

She said, 'The *Real Housewives of New York* are on TV.' So she was going to stay up and watch that; luckily by now the incident with the prodding in the back on the sofa was long forgotten, so I said I would go to sleep in the spare bed again, she was OK with that.

Being the perfect wife she tucked me into bed, gave me a kiss and turned off the light. I snuggled down hoping sleep would come quick because I needed it. It took five minutes before I felt a prod on my back, here we go again, I look under the bed and saw something scurry out of the other side into the wardrobe, I turned the side light on and gingerly looked inside the wardrobe and adjoining wardrobe; nothing, not a thing had been disturbed.

I went back to bed and lay there with the light on, waiting to see what would happen. The next moment I get a long push from under the bed, I actually found myself talking to the presence: 'Please, not tonight, I'm shattered.' I realised how stupid this was, I was talking to a shadow. Again, I went to look under the bed when a hand appeared, not a human hand, but something I would describe as a robotic hand, fingers and thumb were there but they were like metallic rods attached to a larger rod as an arm. It quickly grabbed the TV controls off the bed side cabinet and disappeared under the bed. I lay there listening to the punching of the buttons on the remote control, lucky enough Pat had turned off the plug for the TV so that the standby light didn't annoy me. I plucked up courage to look under the bed and there was the hand and arm but attached to a dark shining body of sorts. I lay there in bed wondering what the hell do I do, the presence was tangible, do I call Pat? I didn't do a thing, I listened to a rhythm being played on the controls, the same rhythm that was coming from the wardrobe. I got out of bed and slid the two wardrobe doors together so that I had a complete view of the inside. It didn't take long to realise that the keys on the digits on the wall safe were being controlled by the TV controls, they were sounding in unison as an imaginary hand pressed them.

I honestly did not know what to do, I was stuck to the spot in between the bed and the wardrobe just looking down at the bed and then the key pad on the safe. Then suddenly out of the wall came a similar body to that under the bed, no head just a body and arms and hands. It somehow stuck a box to the wall with a keyboard on that was far bigger than any computer keyboard and quickly started tapping keys making beeping noises that were not in unison with the noise coming from under the bed.

I wanted to run and hide but where, do I tell Pat all or do I just go into her bedroom? I quickly decided to go to her, I bottled the idea about telling her all, it would take too long, so I said just come into the bedroom a minute and see if you can hear a knocking sound. She came in and the knocking had stopped, I looked and the keyboard was gone, along with the presence under the bed.

She said, 'Are you alright, do you want to sleep in my bed, shall I get you some tea, what's up with you?' The only thing I could think of was saying was it must have been a bad dream. I went back to bed and for the second time that night she tucked me in, turned off the light and said, 'Shout if you want me.'

I just lay there in the dark, just wondering what would happen next, five then ten minutes passed, nothing, no sound, no dark shapes, nothing. Twenty minutes must have passed when the telly purred, no channel just a message written in yellow text.

WE DON'T LIKE HER.

Chapter 6

Did I sleep? I don't know, the night just became a whirl in my brain, nothing made sense; did I see body forms or was I imaging them? No, they were too real for my imagination, they were there. But why the message about Pat, why don't they like her, why don't they reveal themselves to her, what the fuck is going on?

I took Pat in a cup of tea, and she was concerned how I had been acting. 'Do I feel I have a fever?'

'Let's go down the doctor's and have a chat with him see if he can help.'

I needed some time on my own not with the doctor or Pat. My headache was growing with every breath I took. I said, 'I'm going for a walk down the beach, clear my head,' but in reality I was just buying time to try and sort my thoughts out.

I checked the wardrobe and under the bed, no sign of any disturbance except what I had created, no sign of any fixing for the keyboard in the wardrobe, nothing to help my sanity.

I sat on the rocks overlooking the sea, there was a cool wind blowing onto my face, I actually felt relaxed and not looking over my shoulder for something to appear behind me. The beach was deserted and it would have been idyllic if not for the thoughts flashing around in my head. I need to tell Pat what's been happening and why I have avoided telling her. I wished I had brought pen and paper to write it all down but would just have to trust my memory. I stayed there for what seemed like ten minutes but it was actually an hour. I decided to walk back to the spar; a cup of coffee and a chat about Chelsea would take my mind off things.

The old lady put the bread on and poured the coffee, she held the back page of the paper up to show me Chelsea had lost one nil at home. We talked football and then more football but she then dropped into the conversation that a local band were having a BBQ in the shrubland behind Casa Bora to launch their new song; a lot of the village were going, were we going? I said, 'Probably not but we'll watch it from the roof of the villa. When are they doing this?'

'Tonight,' she replied, already her beer sales were up for the day and she was going to have to re-stock mid-afternoon. I stupidly asked what time it starts, she said, 'You'll know as soon as you hear the first beat of the drums.'

Well my little walk worked albeit for a short time, but my mind had been given a rest from the constant questions I was asking it. Would it be good for a bit of al fresco music with real people present, would the body forms return later that night or would it be a night of peace from the parallel world, who knows, but it had cleared one decision from my head and that was not to tell Pat until tomorrow. It's true, men are cowards when it comes to confronting the truth.

I got home and told Pat about the band and BBQ, her first reaction was, 'I've got nothing in, what about if some people come back for a drink, you've got two beers in the fridge and I've got the last dregs of a bottle of wine. Come on we need to go to Eroski.'

100 euros later and I felt as if we were running the whole BBQ, let alone a few people coming back for a drink.

They started setting up about 4pm, they had a couple of big lights to cover the area and some small path lights all around the BBQ they were setting up. I was surprised how many people they had helping. I thought I would be roped in but no need. The band's instruments arrived and again I was a bit taken back with the numbers, it looked as if there were eight in the band. By 7pm everything was in place and people were turning up; quite a mixture, some old, some young and some families. This was going to be a bit of a push because most of the shrubland contained – as you would expect – shrubs. Most people had torches so the light was quite good, although with the families most of the children were holding the torches so light was going everywhere.

They started practicing, we won't be sleeping through this noise, I thought. We were up on the roof but decided to go and join them as it was getting pretty busy, the food smelt great and we seemed to know quite a few people. With the Spanish and Germans it was more of a nod hello and to the English it was a stop and a chat. We eventually got to the front of the queue and settled for spare ribs and burger with a jacket potato.

The music was good and we were stood with an English family and their friends; we didn't chat about much, only between tracks was it possible to make yourself heard.

The band finished about 10pm, a few of the younger children already asleep on their dad's shoulders. We asked the family we were talking to if they and their friends wanted to come back for a coffee. They all agreed, quite a few people were staying, chatting to the band and every budding drummer having a go at the drums. We made our way back to the villa with a rendering of Bob Marley being crucified by some up and coming teenager.

We all encamped in the kitchen, as always seems to be the norm, beers were the order of the day and after a few the conversation was quite buzzing. The family had lived in Cala D'Or for five years whilst their friends were staying in a villa just down the road and came over twice a year. It didn't look as if they were in a rush to go but I was desperate to go to the bedroom to see what was happening in there.

I opened the door quietly and to my relief no sounds were coming from under the bed or the wardrobe. I was just about to leave when I noticed something sticking out of the duvet and resting on my pillow. I pulled back the duvet and there was the cross that was on the cat's grave, with the word *Gracias* still readable. I put the cross in the wardrobe and went back to the party in the kitchen, I needed that fresh beer and quick. Twice I went back to the bedroom before they left, nothing had changed and the cross was still where I put it.

After all had left we started to clear up but as it was now 1am we decided to finish off in the morning. Pat said, 'Are you sleeping with me tonight for a change?'

'Yes.'

With the aid of a good few beers, I had a good night's sleep with no disturbances, I actually felt pretty good in the morning despite a mild hangover, maybe that was the answer; drink your way through the spirits and the spirits ignore you.

Chapter 7

Motherly Chat

I wondered to myself as I had breakfast, why I hadn't had a visit from my friend, I felt lonely without her to calm me, and today I had to tell Pat the whole story including the presence of my friend from many years ago.

It was the year that I passed the 11 plus that my mother said she wanted to have a chat with me. She was so proud that day I started Grammar School, with my new uniform and cap, which she had worked extra shifts to pay for. I was the only kid on our whole council estate that passed the 11 plus so I took no end of stick from the rest of the gang. I could handle the stick but it was the fact that Whitchurch Grammar School was a rugby only school that annoyed all my mates; it meant that when they picked sides over the park for endless games of footie I was the one picked as an afterthought now that rugby was my first sport.

I remember that first sports session at school, the teacher was on exchange from America, New

York. He was going to be in charge of us for the next two years, this was Whitchurch Grammar School's first step into the big time, no school before had an exchange teacher from another Country, let alone America. Our games session was always long and we had no end of other teachers from other schools coming to look at his methods.

That first day he introduced himself and told us his background and that he would be mainly taking us for fitness, rugby and American football, something that none of us had really ever heard of; rugby league was a new concept let alone American football, there was no Sky sports then to show us the Super Bowl.

Mr Pattern was about forty and spoke in a broad American accent, which I later found out was quite harsh due to his New York upbringing. He was very physical which showed itself on that first session. I remember his words well: 'Now most people know this is a rugby school but I believe some of you prefer football, let's see how many, those who want to play football step forward.' There were about a dozen of us out of thirty. 'Right, so you want to play football; bend over.' We all looked at each other strange as he went off to fetch a sack, we were all in a line bending down not seeing that he was pulling out a baseball bat from the sack. The bat was cut in half length ways, that left a flat surface.

He stepped forward and shouted at the first lad, 'Say after me, I never want to play football again.'

The poor lad timidly said this and Mr Pattern said, 'Louder or you get two swipes.'

The boy responded by shouting the line, 'I NEVER WANT TO PLAY FOOTBALL AGAIN.' He then took an almighty smack on his arse from the baseball bat.

Mr Pattern went down the line, I was sixth in line, each time he wanted the boy to say it louder, each time the boy got a swipe from the baseball bat. By the time it got to me I more or less screamed, 'I NEVER WANT TO PLAY FOOTBALL AGAIN!'

He said, 'Good,' before he whacked me with the bat.

After his macho start, he then shouted at us to stand up straight, and then ridiculed us in front of the class, saying how we all had tears in our eyes and were shaking as he approached us. Bloody right, we were wetting ourselves, in fact I think John Davies did wet himself. Mr Pattern then proceeded to tell us in a very loud tone, that we were never to mention football again in his lessons and if we did the baseball bat would be coming out again.

I told my mother that night and she dismissed it saying a good whack never did anyone any harm; who would have thought that forty years later, Whitchurch produced one of the best football players in the world who captained the International side, but then again they produced a great rugby player who also captained the international side – nothing to do with Mr Pattern.

It would be interesting to see how he would be viewed in the present day, a possible psychopath I would imagine because that baseball bat was used quite often and he always showed a great deal of enthusiasm when it was needed.

The day came when my mum wanted a chat. I felt awkward as we sat down at the kitchen table and I think she felt the same. She started telling me where I was born; Number 2 Heol Booker, a flat just around the corner from where we lived then. It was a difficult birth and not everything went right, I was 11 and found this conversation hard but she carried on; I think I was just staring at the floor.

'You had a sister, she was born minutes before you but she was dead. You were twins but she never survived childbirth.'

I look back now and realise that I should have asked loads of questions but never did, I was too far out of my depth and my comfort zone. The only thing I could say was, 'Yes, I knew.'

Chapter 8

My mother asked me what did I mean, why did I say that. I tried to explain and made a right hash of it, but then again when you are eleven how do you explain such things?

I started with the fishing down on the river Taff and gave her the full story; she said she had heard the story from Mike Williams' mother but she hadn't mentioned that I was involved. Typical Mike, no doubt he had turned things around to make himself look the hero but I had not told him about my friend's appearance so this was never passed on.

My mum asked me to go on, so I told her about the day I took Flash down the old canal for a walk and to fish for tadpoles. The canal was used for bringing coal from the coal pits further up the valleys down to Cardiff docks. It had become redundant over the years and only about a mile of it was left, all overgrown and disused except for the odd dog walker or tadpole fisherman; I was both.

About half way along there was a small broken bridge which took you into a small field with three trees that had fallen down. For youngsters my age it was a great place to meet up for a game of footie, for older kids it was an ideal location to take your partner and start exploring the seedier side of their relationships.

I sat down on one of the trees and opened my bounty bar, Flash was lying by my side when he got up and went around the side of the tree wagging his tail. I followed him and behind the second tree was a guy smoothing Flash and telling him what a good boy he was. He beckoned to me and I went over, he asked where my usual friends were and were we going to play football. I told him I was just walking the dog, he sat down and we started chatting, can't remember about what but mostly fishing and had I seen the frogs further up the canal, only he knew where they lived. I was interested but I was also aware something had changed. I felt as if he was looking at me differently, but I also felt that I was being looked at by someone else.

It was my friend, very faded but clearly her, she shook her head and kept pointing to the way home, the man grabbed my arm and said, 'Let's go to the frogs.' She kept shaking her head. I made an excuse that he was hurting me and that my friends would be along any time, he called me a fucking liar and said if I didn't go with him he would drag me there. The presence moved towards Flash and it looked as if she had entered his body. Flash barked and bit his ankle and kept trying to bite his other one. I ran and managed to get over the bridge and then Flash came running. He got over the bridge and we legged it but the man did not follow but shouted obscenities at us both.

The next day Mum told me that a man had escaped from Whitchurch mental hospital and was found hanging from a tree that overlooked the clearing. I never went back there even if the street boys were going down there.

My mum cried, she said they were going to call her Mary, she asked if she was blonde like me. She showed me some photos of me when I was five and the resemblance was uncanny. My mum cried for quite some time and just cuddled me, 'We must never tell your dad, he wouldn't understand,' and we never did.

Two months later my mum had a nervous breakdown, the doctor told my dad that she needed to stay in bed and take some tablets; I suppose they were sedatives of some sort. I was told not to go into the bedroom, that my mum was ill and didn't want to see anyone. It took her six months to get her life back and we never ever talked about my sister again.

Chapter 9

Facing up to the truth

I never called her Mary, it didn't feel right but boy do I wish she was around at this moment in time, today I was telling Pat everything.

We walked down to the Hotel Leo, a small German Hotel that stayed open the whole year. I had suggested this because we would be the only ones there and I think I would find it easier to talk about things in a neutral place away from the villa. I felt nervous and I wasn't sure how to start things, so went into things in a clumsy way, saying, 'I have something to tell you that you are going to find hard to believe.'

For the next two hours and three lattes I talked, Pat listened, only asking the odd question. I started with the beheading of the cats, the pushing in the sofas, the body forms in my bedroom and all the other things that had happened. I said I have the cross still in the wardrobe, and explaining Mary was quite hard, yes, I did use her name; but Pat listened intently. I did not tell her about the note on the TV.

I finished and waited; Pat said, which I suppose was the only thing she could say, 'I don't know what to say, I want to go back to the villa and sit in the sun.'

No words were spoken in the ten-minute walk back. We sat on the patio and she asked to see the cross, I went and got it; was it proof that she needed or was it something to ridicule me with? The latter was correct, she said it looked like my writing; I denied it but agreed that it could be an explanation that would put her mind at ease.

'It's a lot for me to take in, if you had said it was haunted it would be far easier to believe. At the moment I have a husband who has a spirit sister, has been in contact with life forms that cannot be explained and that he believes exist. I would say it's a psychiatrist that you need to talk to. Not me. I'm going to lie by the pool.'

I sat on the patio not knowing what to think or do with myself. I had told her everything and was relieved but at the same time thought, do I need to see a psychiatrist? The afternoon was due to take a turn for the worse.

'Do you want a cup of tea? I'm going to get a beer from the fridge, I'll bring it over when it's boiled.'

I sunbathed for about an hour, not relaxed waiting for Pat to say something, but nothing came, she just lay there, ignoring me.

I kept hearing laughter from the shrubland but could not be arsed to get up and see who it was. I went to turn over on my back when I saw someone leaning over the fence trying to break a branch off one of our trees. I ran over to them and they just laughed and disappeared. 'Bloody cheek,' I said as I returned to the sun bed.

Ten minutes later, a different arm was hanging over the fence, the owner was wearing a check shirt. Again I went over and said, 'What the bloody hell are you doing?' Still no reply but a female giggle came through.

I tried to see over the fence and although there was no one there, there was a large group gathered around a mound of rocks. I called Pat and said look at this lot, bit worried what they are going to do with the rocks. She couldn't see, the fence was too high, I got a patio chair and she could see no one. I looked again and could clearly see a group standing there. We went up to the roof of the villa and neither of us could see anyone, even more strange the mound of rocks had gone. Pat said, 'You're imaging things again, sit down and have your beer.'

I couldn't relax, I just sat on the patio, a woman climbed over the fence and started to break a branch off. I walked over to her but as I drew close she literally walked through the fence! Now I was going mad, no point telling Pat, she was already close to blowing a fuse about having to go up onto the roof just to prove a point.

I went up to the roof and there were people milling around, the mound of stones was back and an area was roped off. I saw the woman who was just in our garden so I decided to walk around the back and confront her. There were a good 20 people but the woman in white and black had disappeared. I stopped to ask someone but then noticed no one was talking, just laughing. I felt spooked and just went back to the villa but I felt a strong presence, although Mary did not appear.

I told Pat that I had gone over to the shrubland and people were there but she had no interest, in fact her only comment was, 'Why don't you go inside and get away from them.'

I sat on the patio and just stared into space, not saying a word, listening to the mocking laughter coming from behind the fence, the fence that people could walk straight through. The laughter got stronger, annoyingly louder, then an arm came over the fence then another about three feet further down the fence, both trying to break branches off the olive tree. Were they trying to get at the olives? I don't know but I went across to grab them and they pulled back. I then shouted, 'Fuck off!' The laughter stopped, I got the chair and as I stepped on it, this head appeared over the fence. Our faces were about a foot apart but this was no ordinary face, it was grotesque and in the form of a rhino. I immediately knew it was rubber but it scared the shit out of me, 'What the fuck is going on, who are you? Just fuck off.' I got off the chair and stood back, I could feel I was trembling both with fear and anger. It had gone quiet, I went back to the patio and sat there just staring again.

Lucky enough the gardener, Heiko, arrived to spray some of the palm trees that had developed some sort of infestation; he was German but spoke very good English. He had brought a massive industrial crop sprayer so he needed a hand moving it around the pool. It was bloody awkward and very heavy, in fact I did think this is too heavy for me but I knew I had to man up and not show I was struggling. It took him about an hour and it was good to have his company; it took my mind off things and broke the icy silence between myself and Pat.

It was now about 7pm and Pat was getting ready to go out; I was worried that we would sit around a table and the conversation would turn to my state of mind, which would no doubt lead to an argument and one of us storming off, probably me, I know what I saw.

I made an excuse and said, 'My back was hurting can we just stay in and watch TV?'

'OK but no more phantoms in the night malarkey.' I agreed but I also realised that my back was hurting quite a bit, I know I tweaked it as we lifted the crop sprayer down the steps but thought nothing of it at the time.

I lay on the bare floor to take some of the sting out of my back while Pat made a mix and match meal with cheese, tomatoes, bread and onions. I sat up and ate the food but was starting to feel a bit dizzy and strange. I quickly had to get up and ran to the toilet but didn't quite make it, I puked in the bath and on the wall. I puked again and it was the strangest green colour I have ever seen. I needed to sit down and quick, I sat on the loo, Pat came in to see if I was alright but had to go back, the smell was horrible and the sight was not too good either. It was like a scene from *The Exorcist*.

Chapter 10

I cleaned myself up but could not yet face the mess in the bathroom. It was horrible, my back was hurting more than ever so I again lay flat on the floor.

Pat was worried now and wanted to call the doctor, she thought I was de-hydrated and that was causing my sickness and hallucinations. I replied shouting that, 'There were people there, I can show you where the branch was broken off.'

'No, just lie there and I will get a bucket.'

I was feeling awful but at least some of the pain was easing from my back. I decided that I had better try and make a start on the bathroom. I turned the shower spray on but the mess had congealed and the smell was horrendous. I struggled on for about thirty minutes and made some headway but I was knackered. I chucked bleach everywhere and would give it another spray later.

Again I lay on the floor for a good while but as I got up I saw people sat on the patio chairs. I called to Pat, her immediate reaction was, 'For God's sake Mike, here we go again, there's no one there.'

'But I can see them, look, let's both go out there.'

We did and I touched one, a solid figure. Pat could still not see them, we came back in, we argued and she relied on the old favourite, 'We are seeing a doctor tomorrow, I am going down there now to get you some Dioralyte, you're de-hydrated.'

She left and I lay on the bed. The next thing there were noises as the window and the steel shutters were forced open, two lads climbed through the glass window, I shouted at them but no reaction, they walked through the house and straight through the patio windows to join their friends.

Pat arrived home and I told her what just happened and showed her the forced shutters, she coolly remarked, 'Why if they can walk through windows do they need to force the shutters?'

I tried to explain it away by saying, 'They are metal, perhaps they cannot get through that.' She ignored me and poured the Dioralyte out, I drank it and ran to the loo – I was sick again.

'Look, I'm calling the doctor.'

'No, leave it till the morning, I'll be better after a sleep.' As if I could.

It was 1am and I was just lying there I heard this noise outside the front window. I ignored it to start with but then it became annoying – it was a truck engine revving high. I got up and went to the front door; I could see through the glass that there was something out there. I unlocked the door and there was a tipper truck offloading sand in the road. I went over to it and said to the guy, 'What are you doing at this time of the morning?'

He said, 'Heiko wanted it,' and drove off.

I was just glad the noise had stopped otherwise we were going to face annoyed neighbours in the morning. I went back to bed and then I heard banging out the back. Again I got up and went to see what was going on. It was dark and in my haste I forgot that the patio was stepped down; I tripped and hurt my knee. Swearing, I got up and went to the front of the house, opened the gate and went into the shrubland. There were six people there all in T-shirts and shorts; they had built a small farm paddock. There were two ponies, peacocks, a pig, loads of chickens and ducks; I turned to the six people who were laughing but not talking.

I said, 'Where's Heiko, what the fucking hell is going on, who are you, where's Heiko again?' No answer, they just stopped and carried on.

This was all too much for me, I went back to the villa and then realised I had locked myself out. I had to ring the door for Pat to open it. She eventually opened it, 'Mike, tell me what is happening to you, I can't go on like this.' I went to bed not knowing what to say; I was fucked up.

Chapter 11

I lay in bed not thinking about anything in particular as my mind was so fucked up; clear thought was impossible.

The noise started slowly, it was coming from the wardrobe, the tapping like before but coming from both ends of the wardrobe. I looked inside and there was a male in a long leather coat tapping into a keyboard. I tried to talk but nothing came out, I looked down the other end and there was a woman in a yellow blouse and black skirt tapping into a similar keyboard. I managed to say 'Will you both talk, please, my wife thinks I am going mad.' The woman flicked her head towards the TV and there in yellow writing were the words: **She's not a believer, NO.**

I went to get Pat and then thought, what's the point, she won't see them, another message on the TV: **WE DON'T LIKE HER.**

I sat on the bed and pleaded with them to tell me what was happening but they said nothing, just carried on tapping at a furious pace. A coloured girl in a black and white dress appeared; she was carrying two files and gave them to the man in black. Something registered in my mess of a brain that they were all about the same age, whereas the people on the patio were much younger, early twenties, totally irrelevant but it was at least a thought – something I had been incapable of.

Again, I realised that we were totally exposed; I had the passports, money, driving licence everything in my drawer. I got hold of them and decided if they didn't like Pat I would go and sleep in her bed and take all the documents with me. I opened the door and went to the lounge, she was sat there with a group of people watching the telly.

I asked her to come to the bedroom, 'Who were those people?'

She looked at me and said, 'Mike, there is no one there, we have got to sort this out.' I told her they were in my bedroom and I wanted to sleep with her, I showed her the documents and she put them under her pillow and went back to the TV.

I lay in bed quite calm away from the constant tapping, Pat came to bed and there was an almighty explosion followed by the sound of rockets. Pat went back to the lounge; she said, 'Someone is letting off fireworks in the shrubland.' She came back to bed and said, 'Try and get some sleep; you're safe with me, maybe they don't like me.'

Chapter 12

Pat's Story

I had never known Mike like this, he was always so positive, nothing was a problem, people went to him with problems and he usually came up with an answer, this was not the person lying next to me with eyes wide open, just staring into the darkness.

I must have dropped off but woke up when Mike was at the side of the bed trying to put my shoes on. 'What are you doing?'

'I have a meeting with Lee in 30 mins, need to get ready.' He walked out of the bedroom. My mind was already made up; I was getting a doctor.

'You sit down and wait while I get ready.' He sat there on the sofa just staring, I phoned both the 24/7 doctors, neither answered. I chucked on my trackie and decided that I would have to run down to the village and wake them up. I looked at the clock and it was 4am.

I told Mike to sit there and wait for Lee, he said nothing. I locked the front door and ran to the village; neither doctor answered their door. Panic had now set in; adrenaline was pumping at a huge rate of knots. The Hotel Leo, it must have a concierge, I carried on running, got there and there was a guy manning the desk, his English was good, although he could not understand why I was asking him for a doctor when I was not staying in the hotel. He eventually gave me a number, I rang it and a doctor answered. I gave him a brief breakdown of the situation and he said, 'I will come over straight away, you are about twenty minutes away, stay at the hotel and I will pick you up there.'

I opened the villa door worried what state Mike would be in but he was sat where I left him still waiting for Lee. Being the perfect gentleman he went to stand up to shake the doctor's hand but couldn't get out of the chair, his whole body had gone weak; the doctor immediately thought it was a heart attack but changed his mind after initial examination but still said we must get an ambulance immediately. The doctor asked, 'Do you have medical insurance?'

I said, 'Yes.'

Then the doctor said, 'Okay I will phone the hospital in Porto Cristo.'

I travelled with Mike in the ambulance relieved that I had professional people in charge but the twenty-minute journey lasted a lifetime with tension in the ambulance increasing. We reversed back into the A&E entrance and Mike was taken out on the bed. The receptionists spoke to the ambulance crew and they all realised that Mike was in a distraught state and immediate attention was required, but of course the first thing they wanted to know was about the medical cover. This was the last thing I wanted to do but they could not do anything until approval was given by the insurer. I gave them the AXA policy and the claims girl got hold of them straight away. The signs were not looking good, there seemed to be a problem; AXA had said that we were not covered for overseas medical treatment. I took the phone and said I have the policy in front of me and it clearly states that we are covered, in fact it is highlighted. The girl on the phone said, 'I'm sorry, our records state differently and that you have no overseas cover, only full UK cover.'

'But my husband is dying and we are arguing about a piece of paper,' I protested.

'Sorry, my system will not allow me to override such things and I'm afraid that I cannot help you further,' with that she put the phone down.

I could not believe what had happened, sheer panic now set in. Was I going to lose Mike over some clause that I could clearly see was highlighted yet the computer said no? I wanted to phone back but I remember Mike saying we also had a policy with the HSBC Bank. I phoned them and crying I explained the situation, they wanted such things as our online banking pin, a memorable place, our dog's name and some other form of security question. I said, 'Look, my husband is dying, I am in such a state I couldn't even tell you what day it is let alone answers to all these questions.' I now remember saying for god's sake we have had five dogs, which one's name is recorded I have no idea, I can't ask my husband because he is in no state to talk. Luckily, and I say this again LUCKILY, the man at the other end took pity on me and calmly asked for my name, account number and card number, thank god I had the sense to have brought all this. I gave him the details and I could hear him tapping away on his computer.

After what seemed like an age, he said he could confirm we have cover and he can give the hospital the go ahead. He said he would phone me in about three hours to see what was happening. I thought I would never hear from him again, and handed him over to the receptionist who needed the claim details to proceed.

Without waiting for the admin to be done, they took Mike away and left me on my own to sort out the rest of the details. When the admin was done I joined Mike in the A&E ward; he was wired up to various machines with nurses around him. I sat near him making sure not to get in the way. I noticed another person arrive quite casually dressed with jeans and a t-shirt on. He was obviously someone important as the doctor immediately stopped what he was doing and went over to him, leaving a nurse to take further blood out of Mike.

They talked together and a nurse joined them, all the time throwing glances at me. The nurse came over and asked me to follow them; we went into a side room and the doctor who had just arrived started talking. He could not speak English so the other doctor translated.

'Your husband is seriously ill and we need to operate immediately, we cannot delay.'

I pathetically replied, 'I need to phone the kids to tell them.'

The doctor replied, 'We must go ahead now, we do not have much time, please phone your children while we operate, I cannot stress how serious this is.' Then they walked back towards Mike. They were taking him down to the operating theatre and I followed by his side. They stopped me as they were about to enter the sterile area. I kissed Mike on the cheek and held his hand; he had never had an operation before and even sedated I could see the fright in his eyes.

I stepped back and allowed them to progress. As they entered the area Mike was under complete sedation and the anaesthetic had completely kicked in. He then disappeared into the operating theatre and I was alone. I went and sat in the waiting room.

Chapter 13

I sat there like a zombie, the only thought going through my mind was how the woman from AXA could just hang up the phone with a polite sorry and say we cannot help on this matter.

Ten minutes or more passed and a sense of loss and helplessness prevailed. I then remembered I hadn't phoned the kids. I dialled Rhian's number and trying to be calm I tried to explain the situation, however, it was useless as the tears had set in and it was a hysterical rather than a calm conversation. The same with Lee but he managed to say he would arrange flights now and let me know as soon as possible.

I had given up religion when my father died but I prayed and prayed that Mike would pull through. More and more words that I didn't take in at the time from the doctor kept coming into my head, if we had left it he would not have made it through the night, the operation is three hours long and we hope we have enough time to perform it; what did they mean? Does Mike only have three hours to live? And so it went on, I just sat there with my head about to explode.

They could not understand why Mike showed no sign of pain, they kept asking me this and although I kept running through events in my head not once had Mike said he was in pain.

The phone rang and I went into a state of panic, I couldn't function to answer it, so I missed the call. It rang again and this time I managed to get it. Lee said they had booked flights and were on their way to Gatwick – they should get to Mallorca at about 9.30pm. I didn't say much except to say, 'I need you both.'

The waiting was awful; there are no words to describe it, just going over the same things time after time, with always the final thought – would I ever see him again. I constantly looked at the clock, but there was little or no movement. I would get up and walk around; I would sit back down and immediately get back up and walk again. Nurses offered me tea, I accepted, did I drink them, I don't know, my body was functioning but my mind was certainly not. I was in a state of shock and just wanted to speak to the doctor.

It was 10pm when he walked over to me his face not giving anything away; talk, please talk, say anything but please talk to me.

He sat down alongside me and started by saying that the operation was completed, although they did not know if it will be successful. He told me that Mike was extremely ill and they would have to put him into an induced coma for at least three days; this was to shut down the body and allow it to concentrate on the acceptance of the operation. I had so many questions to ask but none came forward, I asked the main one – 'Will he live?'

The doctor replied, 'We don't know he is very weak and septicaemia and pneumonia had set in.' It was a matter of waiting and allowing the drugs to take effect. It was not the usual doctor's speech, there was nothing positive to grab hold of and hang onto, the translation from Spanish to English did not allow for that. The doctor said I could see him when he was fully set up on the intensive care ward, I thanked him and off he went.

I was taken to the intensive care room but first I had to go through the sterile unit where I had to wash, fit a gown on along with covers for my shoes, mask and hairnet. I was then allowed to enter the room; little did I know that this would become the ritual twice a day for the next three weeks.

Entering the room, I was scared; seeing Mike I was terrified. He had so many tubes and wires attached to him but it was the look on his face where his mouth was prized wide open with the ventilator, he looked in pain despite being in a coma. I wanted to kiss him but the nurses said not to but they let me hold his hand. I could not speak at first but gradually offered words of comfort. Whether it helped Mike I don't know but it helped me knowing I was doing something.

I was there about an hour when the nurse said, 'There is someone at reception for you.' I quickly disrobed, washed again and hurried down to reception.

The kids had arrived at 11pm; we all hugged and cried at the same time, no questions were asked, we just needed each other.

Chapter 14

They wanted to see their dad straight away but the nurses were having none of it, it was too late but after what I had been through nothing was going to stop us. Eventually they let two of us into the room and then we could swap. Both the children were quiet when they saw Mike, it was not a nice sight and seeing the man that had been the rock of the family for so long, so helpless, came strange to them. Neither overreacted but you could see their sorrow and how frightened they were.

They allowed Lee and Rhian about ten minutes each, after that we left and said goodnight at reception and got a taxi back to the villa, all of us extremely knackered and emotionally drained.

The next day we did the practical things, they unpacked, late breakfast and sort out a car for the week ahead. Lee and Rhian walked up to the car hire showroom and managed to get a bog standard Citroen C4, although it did have air con, something we needed even though it was now late September. Lee, not having driven in Mallorca before, did not make the greatest of starts; he stalled, the second attempt not much better as he bunny hopped half way down the exit slope. They both left the compound rather red faced.

By the time we got the car back at the villa it was visiting time so we drove up to the hospital knowing that Mike would still be in a coma but we would be able to talk to the doctor and ask the questions I couldn't take in the previous night.

The reception staff seemed genuinely glad to see us; there were two visiting slots 1pm-2pm and then 7pm till 8pm, they were very protective over these times and there was no chance of adding a few minutes on here and there.

Again they only allowed two people in at any one time, so myself and Rhian went in first. I knew we would get used to the sight of Mike just lying there with so many tubes coming out of his body but it still brought tears to our eyes straight away. Despite not knowing if he could hear or not we both prattled on about nothing of any significance. We both took turns holding his hands but with no recognition on his face it was hard to believe that we were doing any good. Lee changed over with Rhian and again we both prattled on – I think the weather was the main topic of conversation and Lee chucked in a couple of rugby results.

The room was a high dependency intensive care unit. It was completely white, even the one chair that I had to sit on. There were twelve drips hanging down from an overhead station. I counted them every day, as if hoping any removal of one would be an indication that Mike may have been recovering. The bed itself was surrounded by monitors. These were for breathing, heartbeat, pulse and some things that were explained to me, but I didn't take the details in. He looked like a mess of cables, you couldn't see where the body ended and the cables began, everything seemed to be entwined together. The worst thing was the ventilation tube prizing Mike's mouth open. He looked as if he was choking continually. The nurse station had constant visual contact but they still came out to see him every five minutes; constantly checking all the monitors.

We spoke with the doctor after our hour visit and thankfully his English was very good. He explained that Mike would be kept in a coma for three days, they had shut his body down while it accepted the operation; they wanted this to be the sole function and re-assured us it was the best chance of survival. The doctor stressed that this would be a crucial time and again went over how serious Mike's condition was; he did not at that time give us the full facts but we later found that there is a 20% mortality rate with this type of operation.

We left the hospital, none of us really talking, I suppose we were all shell shocked about the level of inactivity from Mike; just a body lying there, not knowing if he could hear us, or knew if we were even there.

It was now about 3pm so we thought we would go for lunch. Lee drove around and we pitched up at this tapas bar, which at first we thought was a mistake as it was full of locals and looked very basic. It turned out to be excellent food with great service; the menu was cheap which was lucky as the last thing we had thought about was stopping to get some money, we scrabbled together enough to pay the bill and leave a tip.

The next three days followed a similar format of two hours a day visiting, a chat with the doctor at some point who would reveal more about the operation on each occasion, but he would not comment on Mike's condition as there was nothing to report. Again, the nurses and reception staff were always extremely helpful and polite and kept us informed of everything taking place.

Chapter 15

On the fourth day we were surprised to enter the room and find Mike awake. Again it was just the two of us allowed in and I felt guilty that I did not rush out straight away to tell Lee that his dad was awake.

Mike could still not talk; the ventilation tube in his mouth prevented any movement of the mouth and he did look in pain from it. Again we talked about nothing but at least we were getting some recognition with eye contact. Lee swapped with Rhian and we went through the same procedure of holding hands, talking continually but not saying anything.

The doctor came for a chat before we left and he informed us that Mike was out of the coma but heavily sedated and would continue to lapse in and out of sleep for the next two days. He said that everything was working alright and it looked as if the body had accepted the operation. He then told us about the exact details of the operation. The hernia had caused strangulation of the intestines within twenty-four hours – some had died and had already purified into just mush. This had caused septicaemia to occur and spread through the whole body, the constant vomiting had led to pneumonia in both lungs and this was causing the whole body life function to close down. They had to cut away about two feet of the intestines and some of the bladder and to make the body stable and to accept the changes.

He was thorough in his detail and gave us a complete breakdown of what had happened. None of it sounded good and we could now see why the timing was so crucial; Mike literally was two hours away from death as the operation took place.

The doctor would not commit to say if Mike was out of the danger period but he did say he would be in intensive care for a lot longer than first envisaged and that not to expect much change in the coming days.

We left the hospital quietly not knowing what to say or do, there was so much to take in, and the shock that we were so close to losing Mike and that we were still a long way from recovery with many pitfalls on the way.

Back at the villa we discussed what I was going to do, it looked as if I was going to be there for a lot longer than we had first thought. Both Lee and Rhian had to go back home at the weekend and they were worried about me having to take a taxi twice a day to the hospital and then coming back to the villa on my own. We decided that the next day we would see if there was a hotel near the hospital that I could book into and stay there until I knew what was happening.

They left me at the hospital and walked down to the town of Porto Cristo. It was a relatively short walk, only about fifteen minutes but there was very little open and very few hotels. The one they found was pleasant enough, it actually sat on the small cove of the bay and had a lovely albeit small sandy beach. They booked me in for three days and went back to the hospital, we did not know at the time that I was going to be there weeks rather than a couple of days.

There was a big surprise awaiting them at the hospital; Mike had had his ventilation tube removed and he could speak. He was very slow with his words and it was painful for him to talk but he tried his best. The kids were not there long as most of their time had been taken up with the hotel but you could see that they were relieved that the ventilator had been removed and the grotesque sight of their dad lying there with his mouth wedged open was no longer just staring at them. It was only when we had our chat that we realised that the removal of the tube had been quite eventful and luckily we were not there to witness it.

When they turned the ventilator off and removed the tube Mike stopped breathing and despite pumping his body they could not get him started so they had to put him back on the machine with all sounds of alarms going. We never really got to the bottom of how they successfully got him off the machine, it was lost in translation, but we believe it came down to trial and error, it had caused much concern with the staff and they looked physically shocked and drained as we were being told.

Despite this worry we came away from the hospital with an upbeat mood, something we had not experienced since Mike was rushed in and although we knew there was a long way to go he did not look as vulnerable as he did with the tube and machine in place.

So back to the villa we picked up some clothes and booked me into the Hotel Felip. Having never stayed in a hotel on my own before I was a bit nervous when I went down for dinner believing the whole restaurant was looking at this sad loner. I took solace in my book along with a casual perusal of the self-service buffet.

The hotel was full of Germans and although I would have no worries about not getting a sunbed first I was flabbergasted how much the outside communal areas smelt of smoke, it was quite off-putting and I tried to avoid these areas so that my clothes weren't tainted with the smell.

That first morning I walked to the hospital and it was a pleasant stroll, mostly uphill but not too tiring. I met the kids there at visiting time and told them about the hotel and that I would be okay on my own; my secret worry was the walk back to the hotel, the area around the hospital was a bit barren but I planned to get a taxi when needed.

Again, it was good for us all to see Mike and for him to realise we were there and for us to talk some sense, something that we had not done before.

Visiting time passed, we didn't see the doctor, good sign or bad, not sure at the time. The kids came back to the hotel with me and I showed them my room and they stayed for dinner. Chat was slightly light hearted but we all knew that they were leaving the next day so it was more gallows humour than anything. We finished eating and they left to pack for their departure and to clean up the villa. I managed to find some UK channels on the TV and sat on the bed and let my brain rest.

Chapter 16

Morning came too fast, the kids were at the hotel, we all had breakfast and then it was time for them to go, they would not be able to see their dad because the plane departed at the same time as visiting hours. Thought I held things together well but in the end there were the inevitable tears and fear for us all. We said our goodbyes and there I was alone, I kept my tears until I got back to the bedroom.

It was actually a nice day so rather than just sit around I went for a walk along the beach even had a sit on the rocks, again in a different situation it would have been enjoyable but not today, I was just wishing the time away until I could walk up to the hospital.

My mobile rang and although I didn't recognise the number I answered to a very Spanish sounding voice, it was the hospital and from what I could understand Mike was having a fit and could I come immediately. I just ran up the hill not knowing what I was going to find or do, adrenaline was certainly pumping by the time I arrived at reception. They told me that Mike had become violent, trying to pull out all his tubes and ranting and raving about things they could not understand.

They ushered me in quickly, he was totally strapped to the bed both arms and legs, his one arm was bleeding where he was trying to break the wrist shackle and he was shouting and screaming at everyone and everything. I took his arm and tried to talk calmly; it had an immediate effect. I just kept saying I was here and everything was alright, again it was comfort talking, with nothing particular registering. It took about five minutes before Mike was just lying there staring into space, not saying a word, his eyes glazed as if he was staring into another dimension. I just garbled quietly talking about the kids, grandchildren even the pigs, just being positive. It worked and in fact I stayed there three hours in total, by then the extra sedation had kicked in and he was in a comatose sleep.

The doctor came and saw me, he was straight to the point and said he was not happy with Mike's recovery and that it looked as it would take far longer before they could allow him to be released for repatriation. He asked if I could be on call 24/7 as it was the only remedy they had to calm him down, they didn't want to keep him heavily sedated as it slowed down his recovery rate. I obviously said yes and in fact offered to move into the hospital. This they declined but said they would call when needed and to ignore visiting times, just come and go as I needed.

There was a TV in Mike's room but it was all Spanish channels, they got an engineer in to retune it to Sky News, but this had a detrimental effect and seemed to cause even more panic attacks with Mike.

For the next four to five days I was constantly spending more and more time in the hospital, the only time they would unshackle Mike was when I was there holding his hand just trying to calm him down. It was not good and I must admit I was totally scared not only for myself but also the staff; they seemed incapable of remedying the situation. I was becoming their main crutch to lean on and my concern grew deeper every day. Mike was talking to people who he believed were beside me, in the room together. He would hold conversations with them and it appeared in his mind they were answering back; it was as if he was in a different world.

My only comfort was the calls I was receiving from home, from both kids, and close friends and family and Kaye, who even offered to fly over to be with me. It was my only sane time when I was on the phone away from the reality of an unreal situation. Rhian had been distraught all week and decided she could take no more and told me she was flying over and bringing the kids; she had booked a flight and would be there as soon as she could.

She caught a taxi from the airport and came straight to the hospital in Porto Cristo; we both cried but tried not to show it so we didn't scare the kids. They were not allowed into the intensive care area so it was very much either me or Rhian spending time with Mike while the other one looked after the kids.

After visiting we picked up a car and Rhian drove us back to the villa for the night; considering she had never driven abroad she did extremely well, although I was not the ideal passenger.

For the first time in three weeks I seemed to have a normal life; the grandkids, Ayla and Caleb were excited to see the pool and to find all their toys stored under the bunk beds. I actually got some sleep for the first time since this bad dream had started.

Chapter 17

The arrival of Rhian seemed to have a very positive affect on Mike, he became more lucid in his conversations and started to make some sense with his comments. I walked in one day and he asked if I had changed my gown, as I had had it on for two weeks; not a big step but a small attempt at humour. He was desperate to see the grandkids but the staff were adamant they were not allowed in. I think we were both grateful of this as it would have been quite a shock to the kids to see their gramps all wired up and lying there helpless; he was still shackled when I was not there but they were taking them off when I was present.

Although things were starting to improve I was still getting out of visiting hour calls asking if I would come in and try and calm him down. It was still pretty traumatic to handle but he would usually calm down after about ten minutes of me whispering to him about the grandkids and how much they missed him and we all couldn't wait until he was out. This always worked but I was so relieved that it never happened when Rhian was there.

I spoke to the doctor after one such incident, basically looking for some moral support and to see when they thought Mike could be repatriated to the UK. The doctor was honest and said that his recovery was improving but they were concerned about his stress attacks, especially for the flight back; they needed at least a clear week of attacks before they could make a decision and to start the planning of the repatriation. To my shock he told me that I would not be allowed on the same flight back as Mike. Before I could gather my thoughts about this his phone went and he had to dash off.

As the news sunk in Rhian and the kids arrived and I put it to the back of my mind but it re-appeared in the early hours of the morning and kept me awake for most of the night. Why couldn't I fly with him, surely I was the best means of keeping him calm? The questions kept on coming into my head but no answers followed. I needed the hours to pass so that I could sit down composed with the doctor and ask these questions.

The next day Rhian and I are in reception waiting for visiting hour to start when the doctor walked by, so I immediately grabbed him and started rattling out all the pent up frustrations of my lack of sleep. He calmly said he would sit down with us after visiting hour and we could talk then about how things would be planned.

I went in to see Mike first just to make sure he was alright to see Rhian. He was sat up talking to the nurse and gave me a lovely smile as I arrived; this was his first real sign of recognition since the operation had been carried out. I did my fifteen minutes and was genuinely surprised how switched on and relaxed he was. Rhian then sat and talked to him and when she came out she said she was also surprised the change in Mike from yesterday, but he kept going on about a rabbit that was in the ward and how the kids would love to see it.

I sterilised my hands again and sat down on the chair next to Mike's bed. He looked a bit groggy and I wondered if he had peaked, but he suddenly came around and was all smiles again. His first words took the smile off me though, 'Wasn't it great that he had seen the rabbit he must be getting better.' I played along and said where was it and he pointed with his eyes to the chair and said it kept running under there. He described it in detail and was genuinely excited, we spent the whole fifteen minutes talking about it and when it was time to leave he grabbed my hand and looked at me and said we are safe now.

After Rhian came out after her fifteen minutes we went looking for the doctor. I asked if he mentioned the rabbit and she said, 'No, but kept saying it won't be long now until we are home.'

We went to the doctor's office and although it was awkward with the two kids, he explained what would happen with repatriation and gave us some indication of when it would take place although this was subject to the next few days and how Mike progressed.

The two main drivers were no more stress attacks and he had to have a solid bowel movement – something he had so far failed to do – this was causing some concern to the doctors but they were prepared to wait.

The repatriation was a nightmare. They would fly three doctors over from the UK to take Mike back, the plane would be small and with the two pilots, doctors and flight staff there, so there would be no room for me. The actual details of the flight would be given to me closer to the date, the only thing the doctor could say was that it would be flying out of Palma, so about an hour trip in the ambulance from the hospital. I realised the severity of this move when I found out that three doctors would be taking part and that there would be a team of eight at the other end awaiting his return.

It only hit me on the way back to the hotel that I would be flying on my own in a separate flight, something I had never done before, another restless night with no sleep.

Chapter 18

Rhian was around for another two days and then it was back to me being on my own, certainly the arrival of Rhian and the kids had not only been a great boost to me but also Mike. He was far more awake and with it on each of our hour long visits. Although he was still wired up to no end of drips and machines, plus the shackles were still present just in case, you could put these to the back of your mind when he was laughing and joking.

The day before Rhian left we went into hospital. Again, I went in first and he was sat up in bed with the broadest grin I had seen for quite a while with a real smug look. 'I've had a poo.' His excitement was tangible and even the nurse clapped, evidently the whole hospital knew but Mike asked them to keep it a secret until he had told me. There I was, tears in my eyes, all over those four little words. I was an emotional wreck and went out and told Rhian Dad has something to tell her. She went in and also came out with tears in her eyes. We both phoned Lee and then Daley, Rhian's husband, and

Tracey, Lee's wife; at this rate it was going to make the ten o'clock news.

After visiting we took the kids down to the beach for a play, it was as if we didn't have a care in the world, we actually felt relaxed, the kids loved it and somehow seemed to realise we were actually happy. Not sure in the history of the world if a poo has ever been so significant!

The next day Rhian and the kids went back to the UK, there were still tears but tinged with some positive thoughts, Mike/Dad was recovering, albeit slowly.

The next three days passed quickly, no more stress attacks, Mike on some form of solids and still having the required bowel movements. My main concern was that he had not been out of bed for over three weeks and that he still had a catheter in with no hint of this changing.

Puerto Cristo is a lovely little place, quite compact and very friendly. I had started talking to shop keepers and word had got around about Mike, the hotel staff had no doubt spread the word as every day I had to go through an endless tide of questions from all, but it was nice and helped the boring hours pass. It was Wednesday and I was on the way to the hospital, window shopping and called into a jewellery store. I was surprised to meet the woman behind the counter as I had met her a few times before in a gift shop near the hotel, she had in fact sold me a few toys for the kids to keep them amused during visiting hours.

We had a good chin wag and she was asking about Mike and any news on his release, sounded like a prison. I said we were still waiting, didn't mention the big step forward with his poo, but somehow I think she knew. She said call in tomorrow and I will have some real English scones and a cup of tea for us.

I walked into the hospital and before I could say hello, the receptionist said, 'Quick, the doctor wants to see you.'

I panicked and kept saying, 'Is everything alright?'

Luckily enough the doctor heard me and came straight out. 'I have good news; we reckon Mike is ready to go home.'

I hugged him and then the nurse, 'Can I see him, does he know, when?' The doctor talked as we walked, if everything went to plan it would be Saturday. Mike didn't know yet, he wanted us both to be there when he told us, I forgot about sterilisation and was only stopped by the nurse because I had also forgot to put my gown on. I needed to calm down. we walked to Mike's bed, the doctor, nurse and me. He looked nervous, no greeting smile, just a look of concern – there were three chairs and we all sat down. The doctor took control and told us that the improvement in Mike's condition was good and that they were looking at repatriation on Saturday. Mike cried, I cried and the nurse followed suit. The doctor remained calm and warned us that things could change but at present the flight was booked, the doctors were on standby in the UK and that tomorrow I had to sit down with Cega, the flight operator and go through all the details, plus arrange a flight back for myself. The nurse and doctor then left us and we went silent, too emotionally confused to talk.

It seemed like a lifetime before Mike finally said, 'Hope they got Sky at the next hospital – it's the first weekend of the European Championship.'

'How on earth do you know that? You haven't read a newspaper or watched telly for weeks.' He said he didn't know but guessed – when I googled it he was right.

The hour passed quickly, we were both making plans that were all going to change tomorrow when I met the flight operator and travel co-ordinator. Never mind for that hour we were excited after 4 weeks of intensive care, we were going home. Just before I left he said, 'I knew we would be safe when I saw the rabbit.' Why did he keep mentioning the bloody rabbit? Please, please no relapse.

Chapter 19

On the way back to the hotel I stopped at the jewellery store and enjoyed some lovely scones and British tea; it seemed as if I was floating although I was firmly sat on the chair, holding the cup and talking incessantly about going home. I thanked my new friend for her kindness and decided to have a quick stroll along the beach. The air tasted sweet and the sea – as if out of respect – was totally calm.

At the hotel I was met by so many smiling faces, they had all heard the news, little did he know but Mike had become quite a celebrity without ever leaving the hospital.

The next day I talked with the Cega travel operator and she informed me that the three doctors had been confirmed and they would be flown over on Saturday morning and would be briefed by the doctors before meeting Mike. The briefing would take a couple of hours, plus they would also see a DVD of the operation. I was impressed but also scared at the length of preparation it would take before Mike would be released. They had not yet decided whether he would be sedated for the trip; this was going to be a last minute decision depending on his state of mind and anxiety.

A decision would also be made on the day whether I would be allowed to see him before his release. I tried to insist that it would be a good calming influence on Mike, but it came down to the decision of the doctors; both the British and Spanish doctors would make the judgement call after their debrief.

The plane would be small, there would be no room for me on board, plus I would have to take Mike's hand luggage with me, they told me all the equipment they would have in place on the plane and although most of it went over my head it sounded an immense list.

It sounded like the equipment would be brought from the UK and would already be in situ on arrival at Palma. Mike and two doctors – one British, one Spanish – would travel in the first ambulance and the two remaining British doctors would travel in the second ambulance along with two nurses who would help with the transition from the ambulance to the plane on their arrival at Palma airport.

The Cega operator then told me that I would have to talk to the insurance department of the company about my flight back. I explained I had a return flight booked but this was four weeks ago.

To be honest, she was not interested – her job was co-ordinating the repatriation, it was not in her remit to look after me.

I thanked her for her time and went back to the hotel to sit on the phone and started trying to arrange my transportation back to the UK. It was slightly confusing to start with; HSBC and Cega had to agree who was in control of this part of the operation. After about an hour I started to get somewhere and Cega were now co-ordinating my transfer home. They were initially saying that they would fly me to Stanstead/Gatwick or Luton. I told them that my original flight back was booked with BA into Heathrow. They ummed and ahhed about this but I kept pushing the point that the longer I was away from Mike the more chance there was of him having stress attacks. Let's be fair, although he was recovering, after four weeks of lying in a bed with no communication with the outside world except for me and the kids, this was going to be a big shock to his system. They eventually agreed that they would fly me back to Heathrow and then started looking for a flight that had a seat available. Luckily enough the 4.30pm flight, that I was originally due to fly back on, had a seat and they booked me in for that slot.

I was knackered, the mental stress took its toll and I just sat there staring into the four walls of a room that had become my home for the last four weeks. I looked at the time and realised that this had taken about three hours and I had better get a move on, otherwise I would miss visiting time.

Not sure if I was much comfort to Mike that night, my mind was all over the place. I knew sleep was going to be impossible that night.

Chapter 20

Saturday had arrived, I had packed, brought some stuff from the villa that I needed to take back to the UK and had phoned the hospital to see if I could see Mike. They immediately said yes and could I come straight away, nothing to worry about but Mike was getting confused and they were concerned that this would lead to stress.

I got a taxi to the hospital; although it was a short walk, I would struggle with two sets of hand luggage and all the necessary documentation that I had accrued over the last forty-eight hours. I said goodbye to the hotel staff and this proved emotional in itself, they all wished me well and said to bring Mike back when he had recovered.

Sat in the taxi it seemed unreal that we were going home and then my nerves started to kick in, I had never flown on my own before, I didn't like sitting next to strangers, and then stupid little things: would I be able to reach the overhead lockers with my luggage, would I find the gate, Palma is a huge airport, shut up head – I was supposed to be going to calm Mike down not add more pressure to the situation.

I arrived at the hospital, put my bags in reception and went straight up to Mike's room. This was totally unreal, there he was sat in bed in just his gown, drips and machines still connected. Had something gone wrong, couldn't he fly, was there a problem? Luckily enough the doctor arrived and we sat down and I blurted out what was happening, I at least expected him to be sat in the chair partially dressed, looking at least as if he was going somewhere. The doctor explained that Mike would be transported to the plane in the bed and it was essential that some of the drips remain in place; the monitors would be removed but he would be re-connected when aboard the plane, the catheter would remain in place and he would be encouraged to have a bowel movement before his journey began – this they could control by drug intake and it would be far easier to have him sat on a bed pan in the hospital rather than on the plane.

The doctor told me to relax, it was all in good hands and had been planned to the finest detail, the unknown was how Mike would react to all that was happening. They were going to sedate him but only lightly to start with, they would see how he progressed through the morning and everything I could do to keep him calm was essential. Mike would leave the hospital at the same time as me, they had arranged a taxi for 2pm for me and Mike would be taken to the ambulance at 1.30pm, it was now 10.30am. The doctor said he would be back every hour to check progress although the nursing staff would be monitoring Mike's condition until his departure.

One nurse brought me a cup of tea and she then told me what would be happening over the next couple of hours, they may have to ask me to leave the room on a few occasions but the rest of the time they would rely on me to help him stay calm.

I sat down beside Mike's bed and we started chatting, he seemed relaxed but also very excited. He cracked a few feeble jokes about always wanting to fly in a private jet, what films they would have, etc. He would have moments of quietness as if he was trying to take in everything that was happening, and to be fair it was extremely busy all around him, nurses that I had not seen before were appearing and disappearing continually, checking various bits of machinery and at least nodding to each other reassuringly. I just sat there talking to Mike, not sure if he was hearing me at times but then at other moments he seemed as bright as a button. I didn't realise until later that not once did Mike ask how I was getting home or was I in fact going home; this was unusual as he knew my fear of flying was intense and in a normal situation he would be extremely worried about me, but this was certainly not a normal situation.

The one thing that stuck in my mind all the time, niggling away whenever I had peace and quiet, was that Mike had not shown any form of emotion since he emerged from the coma. Normally, where the family were concerned and if they had any problems, his concern and emotion would be over powering but there had been nothing to show any feelings in any way. I thought it strange, I had not told the doctors and now wished I had.

The morning went quickly, mainly because of the number of people in and out of the room. at about 1pm I was told this was it and that they would be moving Mike shortly, could I say my goodbyes and make my preparation for the journey. I felt both of us holding hands more tightly than we had done, I kissed him on the lips, it was no point trying to cuddle him, I would never have got out of the entanglement of wires and drips and then I was outside in the corridor, eyes full of tears and a huge hole in my stomach.

I went into the toilet, tried to compose myself and through sheer force of habit put some lippy on. I went out and started saying my goodbyes at reception, everyone had a little bit of English to say, mostly good luck, a few hugs and kisses and then the taxi appeared. The doctors had already said goodbye but still came to see me off.

The taxi driver took my bags and I was off to the airport, I did not see the ambulances leave but assumed they were ahead of us.

Chapter 21

I was shaking as I got out of the taxi at the airport, usually I would just follow behind Mike, but I found the BA desk and checked in. I explained that Mike was flying back separately on a hospital plane but that I had his bag due to lack of room on the plane. This caused great concern and the supervisor was called. She said I would have to pay for Mike's bag as I was only entitled to one piece of hand luggage and I had two. State the bloody obvious, I argued but she and her sidekick were having none of it. I felt myself rising to the argument but then thought I want to just get on the bloody plane and get out of here. By this time, I had attracted another supervisor who also was pretty determined to charge for the second bag. I handed over my card and they took the sum of approx. £20, why had I wasted so much time, but now at least with some fire in my belly nothing was going to stop me getting on that plane.

I don't recall going through the airport, I must have bought a magazine because it was in my hand as I took my window seat, the overhead locker was not a problem as a guy behind me helped me up with the second bag.

I sat down and just stared out of the window praying that no one was going to sit next to me, however, this was short lived as two guys took the remaining seats. I carried on staring out of the window and then suddenly realised that on the tarmac was a small Cega plane with an ambulance next to it. It was too far away to identify anyone on the ground but I did see some bodies getting into the ambulance and drive off. I was now transfixed just looking at this small plane in the distance, I think the stewardess had gone through the emergency procedure but I was not entirely sure.

The next moment the small plane started to move, it was coming towards us, slowly but I could just make out the pilot's shapes, surely this must be the plane that Mike was on. It passed our plane and I kept looking for as long as it was physically possible, I was then trying to see if I could see it through any windows on the other side of the plane but it was not possible.

The engine noise started to increase and we ourselves started to reverse back. We then stopped and waited, I was like a rabbit caught in a car's headlights, just staring at the headrest in front of me whilst gripping both arms of the seat. In my mind I was grateful that the guy next to me had his arms folded and looked as if he was trying to sleep.

We were soon airborne and the worst part for me was over, I wouldn't say I relaxed but I did stare at some of the pictures in the mag I had. They came around with a drink and some food, I was not eating but then realised I had not ate all day. I asked if they had a packet of crisps and they gave me two of the smallest packets I had ever seen, I counted four crisps in one and five in the other; however, they did the job.

We started to descend and the chap next to me said, 'That was quick and pretty smooth.'

My reply was a bit abrupt, 'Not for me.' I then poured the whole story out for the next twenty minutes, from the very start to seeing Mike's plane at the airport – I felt sorrow for him, he took the brunt of all my tension but then the next minute we had landed and were taxiing to the stand.

As soon as we came to a stop he was up and got my cases and then held the people back, explaining to them that my husband was ill and he was on the plane that had landed ahead of us and that I needed to get to him as soon as possible. I didn't want to explain that Mike was going to a different airport, I had probably left that out of my verbal diarrhoea. Anyway, it worked and people stepped aside to let me through, it was a long procession of thank yous.

I had never landed at terminal five and it was a bit daunting, I got confused on their light transit shuttle and ended up going the wrong way to start, although it was only two holdalls that I was wheeling it was not that easy to manoeuvre.

I got onto the right shuttle and ended up going up the steepest elevator I had ever seen, not easy, and I was cursing these bloody holdalls. I got to the top and thought I had better turn my phone on. Immediately it started to bleep for incoming texts. The first one was from Cega; Mike had arrived safely at Blackbushe airport and they would update me as soon as they got the doctor's brief. Great News, they did think they wouldn't make Blackbushe in time so were planning on diverting to Bournemouth but obviously the fuel held out. The next was from Rhian and Lee, they were waiting for me at arrivals, thank God.

I got through the rest of the airport without incident and saw them as soon as I came out of the arrivals door; Daley was with them as well. Big hugs and kisses, tears and happiness, me and Mike were home.

We got to the car and another text came through from Robert at Cega, the doctors had said Mike travelled well, was tired but all was okay, he was now in an ambulance with the doctors on their way to the Royal Berks. We followed suit.

Chapter 22

Mike's Return

So this was Blackbushe Airport; bit of a rough landing – are we on grass, a lot of panic happening, they had eighteen minutes to turn around the plane before the airport closed. The pilot and his co-staff had already said their goodbyes before we landed, they stressed they would not have a moment to spare.

What did I care? They had used the magic word 'sedation' before we left the hospital. Apart from feeling like a patient from *One Flew Over the Cuckoo's Nest*, I wondered how much sedation, are we talking – just a bit of happy juice, or a full medically induced coma? As I had no say in the matter I just lay there and waited for their medication to take hold.

In all honesty, I believe I remember the flight totally but at the time of writing this book I am still coming to terms with some of my interpretations in comparison to what actually took place. The brain is an extremely powerful organ but can be tricked quite easily by man induced drugs and I think we can all relate to that in one form or another.

The trip to the airport was quite uneventful: cracked a few jokes, the doctor checking my blood pressure constantly, some machine bleeping away continuously, temperature being monitored and me just staring at the roof of the ambulance. I certainly wouldn't recommend this mode of transport for a sight-seeing tour. The airport was a doddle, no customs, passport control, or duty free, they just drove straight up to the plane. Then it was the fiddly bit trying to get me from the ambulance with my catheter into the plane, don't forget I had not walked for four weeks and had no feeling in my body, let alone any muscle support.

The plane was smaller than I thought, this was certainly not going to be a luxury trip by any means. One thought that came into my mind was Pat telling me that she could not take my bag, as there would be no room for it. At the time, I said that is stupid, how bloody small is this plane going to be? Now looking around I realised there was so much cramped in there that I was going to be lucky to get on board myself. In my sedated mind I also started thinking, where do the crew go to the toilet? I was okay, I had my plastic bag to wee in but apart from going out of the window I could see no option for them.

I was lying on a gurney, small and pretty uncomfortable, the doctors were working frantically, connecting drips, machines, etc. This had become my standard look and any thoughts that it might change for the plane were soon crushed. I was strapped to the bed and we commenced take off, we didn't hang around taxying around numerous run ways; we were airborne almost immediately. It felt strange, no pilot announcements, no emergency drill and no stewardess announcing that they will be around with drinks and food shortly.

Once airborne, a member of crew came to see me. I say came to see me – he could hardly move away from me. He introduced himself and said he would be taking details of my condition during the flight along with one of the doctors, double admin, but hey, this was an insurance claim. He said, 'We are coming over the bay of Palma, if you raise yourself up the pilot will bank over and you will have a great view before we leave Mallorca.' It was a nice gesture but all I wanted was to get home.

Once at a certain height, who knows what height, as I mentioned, no announcements, things started to happen quite dramatically. The doctors took my blood pressure, temperature etc, etc; all was being recorded by both the doctor and air crew, repeating everything ad nauseum from the doctor carrying out the tests. I just lay there once again looking at the ceiling, thank God for the sedative.

The plane remained busy for the whole flight, the doctors were certainly earning their money and they also seemed to be in contact with the doctors back at the hospital – I would say every thirty mins. It all seemed to be going alright, no panics anyway and I think there was general relief that I had not gone into stress mode – must get some of this medication for the next time I watch Wales play!

The panic arrived as we were coming into land, the pilot was giving out instructions, the doctors were also giving out instructions to themselves, the crew said goodbye to me and stressed to the doctors that we had little time on the ground. I only found out later that we were minutes away from diverting to Bournemouth, Blackbushe appeared not to want to take us but the pilot stuck firm.

We landed, there was no taxiing, the door was opened, tubes were being removed from me, machines disconnected and the pilot and crew had disembarked. I was next to go, again it was quite a task, but in reality I had probably moved less than ten feet and was back on another gurney outside the plane. Being just in my gown I was pretty cold lying there holding my own bag of wee, not a great Kodak moment.

The pilot and ground staff were talking in raised voices, neither party were happy but then the ambulance arrived at the same time as the fuel tanker; both seemed to be jostling to see who could get closer to the plane. In the end, they wheeled me to the ambulance, we all got on board – that's the doctors and me – and along with the ambulance crew it became very crowded inside.

I was strapped in, there seemed to be a backup team taking the medical kit off the plane but they were in a separate vehicle, again raised voices all around. One doctor did a quick visual of me, and asked me some totally irrelevant questions: did I know where I was, how did I get here, where was I going and what day was it. I answered them but did not have a clue what day it was, after being in hospital for four weeks, I couldn't tell you what month it was let alone settle on a day.

After another blood pressure check we were off. It seemed to be quite a while until we got to a lit area, we stopped for some reason and the back door was opened and two random guys looked in – customs maybe?

They didn't say anything and then we appeared to be our way. I asked what hospital we were going to and the doctor that had asked me minutes before consulted with his colleague and then said the A & E ward, didn't he know the answer to the question he had asked or had he forgotten already, his colleague chirped in, at the Royal Berks.

It seemed to take ages to get there, it appeared traffic was bad and I was not sure if this was rush hour or not, more staring at the ceiling.

When we arrived, the ambulance crew joined the doctors and they all seemed to have a role in getting me ready to go. They wheeled me into a ward that was definitely not A & E and we were joined by another couple of doctors and nurses. Lots of admin seemed to be taking place, as my blood pressure, etc was taken. Drips started to arrive and the annoying bleeping machine was connected, I was back to my normal nonfunctioning state, no doubt my sedative had been topped up at the same time.

Someone had told me that Pat had arrived at Heathrow and she was on her way over. In all honesty, up to that moment, I had forgot about her travel and it was only then that I started to wonder how she had managed on her own.

Chapter 23

I was taken to a ward that had about 3 people on it, all connected to various drips and machines, we all looked a sorry bunch. It had probably taken about an hour to get to this ward, I was becoming quite good at judging time. It's strange that without a watch or phone you tend to look for other clues to help you gauge the approximate hour; I was a long way from the crocodile Dundee stage where I could tell the time by the sun, but then again I was spending most of my time looking at the ceiling.

I was tired by now, it had been a long day and considering what I had done, or should I say, others had done around me, I deserved some shut eye, but I was determined to stay awake until Pat and the kids arrived; it was not going to be long.

Looking at the drips that were connected there seemed to be much fewer than I had been used to, was this a sign of recovery? Two particular drip bags seemed to be the most active, they had been changed since my arrival. I asked what was in there, they said it was antibiotics and they lasted 40 minutes a pop. For the next couple of days these would be changed continually every forty minutes and, whilst not painful, it was bloody annoying.

There was no fanfare, but all of a sudden four people appeared at the foot of my bed: Pat and the kids had made it from Heathrow. I remember being surprised that they were all allowed in at the same time. It was good to see the family faces, a little bit of comfort after a stressful day, especially for Pat and the kids, as they did not have the benefit of a shot of sedative.

We talked for a while, Pat about her journey which sounded far more exciting than mine, I threw in some random comments about the lack of films and food on the plane and the fact that the landing was so rough. They didn't stay long, they could see I had peaked so we all said our goodbyes and the kids took Pat home for the first time in weeks. Must have been strange walking into a house that she had not seen for at least eight weeks.

I was monitored quite closely all night, blood pressure every forty mins, along with the change of antibiotic drip; I think I did sleep through a few of the change overs.

The next morning started early, 5.30am. They washed my face, arms and hands, gave me some water to drink and did the usual blood pressure, temperature, etc. I was told that they were moving me later that day to another ward but the doctor would be around first to examine me.

She didn't examine me; she looked at notes, asked me a couple of questions about the flight, was I okay after the landing, why was I so confused about it, where did that come from? I asked her what she meant and she said I was very disorientated because I did not answer the doctor's questions correctly and it appeared to the doctor I did not know what was going on. At the time, I was too far removed from reality to answer her, but two weeks later I gave her a right drubbing about how *she* would react given the same circumstances.

After the visit they then moved me to another ward, this was going to be my home for a little while, a bit quieter than the other two and had a view; alright, it was only the car park, but it was the outside world.

About five days in I had my catheter removed, seemed like a big step to me, but it was one hell of a relief to get rid of it – now I had to learn how to pee again. I had been having physio every day, nothing major just some leg movements hanging off the bed and some weak arm movements. It was now at least five weeks since I had walked and supported my own weight. I was peeing into a urine bottle and the bed pan was still around for number twos, but with no real solids going down these were few and far between.

The nurses told me that they wanted me using the toilet by the end of the week, they would wheelchair me there and help me onto the toilet but then it was up to me. What did Neil Armstrong say? One small step for man, but one giant leap for mankind.

The big day arrived and I passed with flying colours, pun in there somewhere, but boy was I knackered. They told me that the next two days would be the same and then they expected me to walk to the toilet on my own. It's funny that after a major operation, the toilet regime becomes such a major factor in your rehabilitation, not something you think about really.

It actually took me four days before I could walk to the toilet unaided, the sense of achievement was incredible. It then took me a further two days before I could do it twice a day and walk with some confidence. I was on the road to recovery, or so I thought, but the doctors disagreed.

Chapter 24

The one thing I had in hospital was time, so much time, my concentration levels were at an all-time low. Although I had a TV and Pat would bring me in papers and magazines, I could not find interest in either, I would lay there for most of the day and a good deal of the night just going through my mind what had happened, the hallucinations, the events leading up to them. Was I going mad, had the septicaemia set in before the doctors had said and caused these sightings? But then things like the beheaded cat and kittens, the cross from the grave on my pillow, the real people and the imaginary people, the rabbit and the presence of Mary crossed my mind. It was only then that I remembered I had seen the rabbit in the Hospital De Llevant and how at ease I had suddenly felt knowing that Mary was close by. It was like a black hole in my mind waiting for someone to fill in the gaps but with no one coming forward to help.

The induced medical coma scared me, thoughts kept coming back continually, it's obvious that you can shut the body down but the brain carries on functioning at an alarming rate. Could or would they do this to me again, was I being paranoid? But the questions the doctors were asking me daily all revolved around my brain and its capabilities of remembering historical events and what took place in my mind during the hallucinations and the coma.

The coma was easy, I remembered every dream and every time Pat came to see me both in the dreams and in reality, her calming talk at the side of the bed brought me out of the dreams, but the rest of the time I was in a different world.

It was a chaotic and intense world; the doctors and nurses were involved but not as doctors and nurses, they were people taking part in my adventures, and each adventure would be life or death threatening. I didn't know how long they went on but they were in such detail and they involved vast periods of my life, from my early childhood through to my first job and onwards. They also went back into history and from each one Pat saved me and brought me out of the dream and calmed me down, but I knew I was mentally exhausted.

It was only later that I found out that the doctors had to do the same when I was out of the coma and having what they termed 'stress attacks'. They would call Pat and ask her to come in and calm me down. The weird thing is I don't remember these so called stress attacks or Pat coming in to help me. I find it strange that I recall everything in the coma vividly but nothing outside the coma relating to dreams.

It's now six weeks on and everything is still in my mind about the coma experience – is this what the doctors are trying to free up from my brain?

Were the hallucinations part of my brain prior to the septicaemia setting in, were they halluci-nations? No more drugs Doc, let my mind sort this out on its own. Could it?

Chapter 25

Each day I was getting stronger, Pat or the kids would take me for a walk, not far but just to the end of the corridor. I was now on my fourth different ward. The first night I was on my own, from then on in I had a constant person in the bed opposite and the two other beds were for people who were kept overnight and then released the next day.

The antibiotics kept on coming every 40 minutes, but there were less and less tubes connected to my body and those that were, were only in for about thirty minutes. The doctor came every day, the psychiatrist came every other day and in between, various trainees would be with me for periods that would last between ten and twenty minutes.

Each visitor would finish with an A4 sheet of questions, all historical; when did the First World War start and end, when did the Second World War end, when did the first man walk on the moon, who was king or queen in 1930 and then what day was it, what year was it and who runs the country, does anyone know that?

I know for two weeks I failed miserably, even got the present year wrong, but then the questions were starting to be repeated so I was able to answer far more second time around.

By the way, the king was George the V in 1930 and the year was 2014, although now at the time of writing it's 2015, I'm just trying to show off my new found knowledge.

Towards the end of my rehabilitation I was becoming angry at this constant barrage and refused to answer them – I felt like a performing chimp but would get no reward at the end. It seemed such a pointless exercise but the one girl nearly ended up crying because of my refusal to answer the questions, she would not pass her exam, she was so close to tears I relented and answered them.

There were some amusing incidents; the physio nurse showing me how to raise off the toilet after a poo – okay I had all my clothes on but she was stood there with the door open watching my every move along with all the people passing by in the corridor; and then the staff nurse scolding me because I was walking with odd anti slip socks on. I made a joke of it saying I had an exact same pair back at my bed; my attempt at humour went straight over her head and she asked me to return to my bed and put them on. Happy days.

It was in the second ward that for me the cheekiest incident took place. The guy opposite me, aged about forty, was in for a footballing accident. I got on really well with him, we talked sport mostly but he also had a little business going where he was selling football kit. People were coming in to visit him, curtains would go around the bed, and ten minutes later they would leave stashed up with shirts, boots and even a ball. This went on for the whole week but it's not the bit that amused me the most. His wife came in every day, usually for only about ten minutes, she was quite attractive and very pleasant, would always ask how I was and was there anything I needed.

He would then have another female visit him, quite late and she would bring in replacement kit for him to sell, along with a pizza, or kebab and even a KFC the one night which smelt gorgeous. The thing was she would not leave and ended up staying the night sleeping in the bed with him. This did amuse me, thinking not only was he running a business from his bed but he was also getting his leg over on a regular basis, but he also had the cheek to talk to his wife about 10pm every night on the phone, making sure she was okay and wishing her a good night's sleep whilst his lady friend lay beside him.

When I left the ward for my new accommodation he actually got out of bed and came across and shook my hand. I said surely it should be me shaking your hand! we both laughed and I said I would call in before I left to see how he was doing. I never did, it was like a holiday meet where you are always going to keep in touch and never do.

Chapter 26

I now felt we were getting to the serious end bit of my stay, for me anyway, I was feeling more confident and certainly stronger, I was even walking the corridors on my own unaided. I was still getting trainees coming and testing me for blood pressure etc and still asking the stupid questions at the end of their ten minutes. By this time, I was pre-empting this part of the interview by saying that I would talk to them only if there were no questions at the end. Most agreed, the girl who nearly came to tears saw me as a push over and always tried for the question bit but I said I was tired of this and let's just move on.

The doctor visited me that morning and told me that they wanted me to have a full CT body scan and that I would be going down for this later on during the day. When he said 'going down' he was certainly right. The scanner, which was supposed to be one of the most sophisticated and expensive in the UK, was housed in the bowels of the hospital. I was taken down on a bed with just my gown on. As we entered the complex from the lift the cold hit you – as we entered the room where the scanner was housed the temperature dropped even further. They moved me into position, I asked for a blanket but they said it was not possible, then they asked me to lie still. As they positioned me at the entrance of this vast cylindrical hole, I could feel myself shaking – not with fear but the cold was unbearable. The staff then left the room and the machine started to move over me. There was music playing, very loudly, what it was I have no idea but combined with the cold it was not pleasant. The scanner passed over me and then passed back, by the time of the second pass I didn't think I would be able to complete it. They said it would take twenty minutes for both passes and I didn't think I would be able to last the full time. I couldn't see any alarm button and in reality could not move, I had to remain inside whatever happened.

After the longest twenty minutes I have ever known, I was outside the machine, no change in the temperature but the music at least had stopped. They quickly took me to the lift and I was relieved to feel some normality return to the overall temperature. I asked the porter why it was so cold and evidently at first the machine kept overheating and the only way to overcome this was to ensure it was kept in a cold, stable environment. He said everyone complained about the temperature but there was not much that could be done.

Back on the ward, but it took a long time for me to get comfortable temperature wise, plus I had to keep going for a wee – one little side effect they had not warned me about.

About an hour later I was visited by a new face, which asked me various questions about the scan and how I felt during the experience. I kept on about the cold and how I hadn't thought I would make it through the twenty minutes. He said this was a common complaint both from the patients and the staff who worked down there. The staff would work in twenty minute shifts to ensure that their body temperatures did not fall, no doubt a great job during the summer but the winter it must be hell. He said the scanner had cost over £2 million pounds and when it was first installed it had caused them no end of problems because of the overheating and at one stage they had to revert back to the old scanner, whilst they carried out improvements to the new one. I questioned the word 'improvement'.

He asked me about a dozen questions and then said the doctor would see me in the morning with the results, anti-biotic drip re-connected and my life was back to normal, or what had become normal over the last six weeks.

The next day the doctor came around and did have the results; he was quite upbeat and said that the scan showed up no problems and that I had a clean bill of health. I immediately asked when could I leave but then the conversation become serious. They were worried about my state of mind and the psychiatrist wanted to spend some time with me. They were concerned that my memory was confused over the state of events leading up to my emergency admission to the hospital in Mallorca, and that on arrival in the UK I was very unstable at the airport and did not recall the whole chain of events correctly after we had landed. I tried to explain that the whole scene was chaotic, the air crew were panicking over lack of refuelling, the airport was due to close in less than fifteen minutes, the doctors were worried about the non-arrival of the ambulance; in all honesty I was the only one who was calm at that moment in time.

He then questioned the fact that the last time I had seen the psychiatrist's assistant I had stated that I was wandering around in a daze until I saw the lights of the ambulance arrive; this he said was impossible as I was strapped to a gurney, I had also repeated this to another doctor during the course of my stay. He was then quite abrupt and said the psychiatrist would explain all this to me tomorrow but her assistant would be visiting me shortly to review my situation.

So I lay there somewhat confused, I had a clean bill of health, they were happy with my body but not so happy with my mind. I don't know how long I waited for the girl to arrive who was the psychiatrist's assistant, it could have been ten minutes or it could have been two hours, but all the time I was going through my mind trying to recall the arrival at the airport, but more importantly what I had said on previous occasions to this girl and her team. I had not been impressed with her the last time we met, I had asked about having some time at home to see how I would cope outside the hospital environment. I felt perfectly well and it would be a good indicator on the state of my recovery; she felt that this would be a good idea and would put it to her boss, but then when I saw her two days later with her boss, she did not mention it until I brought it up and then she said she didn't think it would be a good idea – her boss agreed. I pointed out that a couple of days previous she had thought that it would be a positive step, but now not so – what had changed?

I kept going over this point in my mind and the fact that I do vividly recall standing up at the airport whilst waiting for the ambulance, watching the chaos that was going on around me, with no doctors paying me any attention until the ambulance finally arrived.

I replayed the fact that I had a clean bill of health but they were worried about my mind.

Chapter 27

The girl and her team arrived, three in al; again two faces I had not seen before. They were introduced and it would appear that they were going to carry out some memory tests on me. I said I was quite happy to do this but I didn't want to get into the question and answer scenario at the end about historic events. They agreed.

The girl was the first to question me, but before she could start, I had a lot of questions I wanted to ask her, especially about the conflict between the different views about the arrival at the airport. She was taken aback by this and very reluctant to continue with the conversation. I insisted and I received some answers. According to the doctor yesterday my body is in good shape but my mind isn't and it seems to stem from my memory of the arrival at Blackbushe airport. I needed to know what was on file about the arrival, but despite making attempts to look through the file she quickly said it was not in that file but she would find out. I said she must have some recollection of this because she fed the information to the doctor and her direct supervisor. She said she would have to consult the other file so that she could comment accurately.

My reply was abrupt and to the point, if she could not remember how did they expect me to remember, after four weeks in hospital being sedated and with no doubt extra sedation for the plane? I said, 'I still stand by mine; and the chaos and panic that ensued at the time was probably never noted.'

I asked other questions about the sedation: was this increased for the trip? Was it administered during the flight? Why was the ambulance not there on arrival? what happened to the three doctors that brought me back – I never saw them again – did they have a debrief when they arrived at the Royal Berks? It was a Saturday night and everyone knows what a hospital is like on a Saturday night. I could have gone on but I was coming up against a brick wall. They were all frantically taking notes but it appeared they were more comfortable with this rather than look at me and provide some answers to my questions.

I changed direction and asked about the CT scans that had been taken both in Mallorca and in the UK, if the MRI scan showed my body was OK what did the CT scans show? Again no direct answers.

I knew at the time that these questions should have been directed at the doctor but I did not have time to compose myself before he had left earlier on in the morning, and these questions needed to be answered.

The rest of the meeting was a very tame affair, they asked some questions, mainly about events leading up to the hospital admission. It was the first time that I actually felt like lying and not being open and telling them the truth, but I contained the anger that was inside me and answered them as best as I could.

I now wanted to leave the hospital as soon as I could, I had been given a clean bill of health and for me that was all I was looking for, I told them what they wanted and the meeting was ended. I asked what the next step would be and they said I would see the Head of Psychiatry the next day. I was told later the exact time of my meeting – 10.30am – something that had not happened before, it was always 'the doctor will see you in the morning', with no time commitment.

I told Pat the time and she wanted to be there, she also had questions to ask. It felt as though this would be the culmination of the last three weeks, in fact the last seven weeks, I don't know why I felt that but in my head this was where my stay in hospital would finish.

10.30am arrived, Pat was sat by the bed and we were surprised when the Head of Psychiatry arrived on time. She was smartly dressed, no tunic or jacket, a nice black and white dress and looking as though she was attending a meeting in the City.

Pleasantries were exchanged, how did I feel etc., it was hard not to say super charged and desperate to get out of here. We continued with airy fairy comments, she was testing the water, I had been abrupt and aggressive yesterday and she wanted to see where I was going to go today.

She said it was good news about the MRI scan and that the doctors were happy about my progress, but she still had some reservations. I had not performed well on the questions that had been asked of me during examinations by her staff. I explained the questions did not interest me and having been isolated in another country for four weeks and cocooned in the Royal Berks for three weeks I was not aware of some of the information required for the simpler questions. The historic questions were explainable, I was basically no good at history and this dates back to school days, but funnily enough, and I wish I had this information to hand then, but since leaving the hospital I have asked many friends the questions that were posed to me and hardly anyone could answer them correctly.

I mentioned that I could tell her my bank account number, my sort code, who was the captain of Chelsea, who was running the country and what I had for dinner last night. She smiled and then brought up my confusion over the arrival at Blackbushe airport. I said, as I had done many times, that I was not confused, I remember it well but my version did not agree with their version, something I had still not seen, she smiled again.

It was only then that I realised she had no notes with her, no files nothing, this suddenly triggered an alarm bell in my mind; I was not going to find out what my file said that was causing them concern.

I tried to push this arrival point further but as like yesterday it went nowhere, I stressed about the panic and chaos but she just listened and did not comment. We carried on our conversation, all very polite, she even said that I had handled the stress and trauma of the event very well, but I felt for some reason that she was holding something back.

I pushed forward saying that I thought I was ready to go home and that I needed to see how I would cope with the outside world. I needed to see if there was something wrong with my mind, but without traction with other people and everyday situations, neither myself or her department would be able to monitor this and gauge if I was progressing. Pat interrupted and said, 'Mike used to have a very responsible job, he ran a company employing over four-hundred people.' I had noticed she had done this quite a few times in our interviews, as if trying to re-assure people that I was not mad.

To my surprise, the psychiatrist appeared to agree with my thoughts and it was time to release me back into the outside world but with a constant review of my progress. With that in mind she wanted to include in my medication a new memory drug, it would be for a short term period of a month and would help me remember events more clearly; would I take part in the trial of the drug. At this point I would have taken sulphuric acid if she had said I could leave.

I agreed and then she pussy footed around, saying I would have to report to my GP about my response to it, I said surely you need to know if it's a trial, she said there would be no need, the GP would monitor things. I asked questions about the drug and was about to say what plus points I would gain from taking it to rekindle memories of things that I believed I was pretty clear on anyway.

She was holding something back and I told her so, she avoided this remark and carried on about the support I would get from the memory clinic and the Cognitive School which I would have to visit every month. She would automatically arrange this and it would start more or less immediately. Again I agreed, I wanted out and this seemed a small step to pay.

I pushed her again about holding something back and she relented. I'm not sure when she would have told me this if I had not kept on, but she very reluctantly said I would not be able to drive whilst taking the drug, plus for two weeks after I had ceased taking it. I smiled and said I had no problem with this, my daughter would be over the moon knowing she gets to keep my car for six weeks, she had already had it since I was in Mallorca.

She relaxed and said, 'Fine, that should be it, the doctor will come in tomorrow and check you over for discharge, I will write up my report and include the provision of the memory drug and that should be it.' She stood up, shook both our hands and was gone.

I wonder to this day whether she would have actually told me about the no driving ban if I had not pushed her or just let me read it in the instructions supplied with the drug.

Looking back, I now feel that the whole conversation which lasted for about an hour was building up to the point of the introduction of this drug to my prescribed medication.

The irony of this point is that it was only two weeks after release that I went for a check-up with my GP and I mentioned the drug and did I need a blood test before I started driving again. He said yes, but there was no hurry, I wouldn't be able to drive until six months after I had stopped taking the drug. I was literally gob smacked, I told him he had it wrong, the psychiatrist had said two weeks. He called it up on the computer and there it clearly said 6 months, if I had taken time to read the instructions with the drug I would have picked up on this sooner, but who reads instructions.

I felt isolated and betrayed, but what could I do, no wonder she was not interested in me reporting the facts of the trial drug to her.

Chapter 28

So the day had arrived, after eight weeks I would be leaving the hospital regime. The day started as any other, 5.30am, anti-biotic drip connected, blood pressure taken, temperature taken and two pieces of toast devoured. I waited for the drip to empty and then got up and went to the loo for a quick pee and a wash and shave.

7am and I was ready to go, now the wait for the doctor. To be fair he wasn't that long; by 9.30am he had checked me, again blood pressure taken, a few questions asked and I was passed to leave. I had intended asking all the questions I had not had answers to but in the end I couldn't be arsed, I did not want to hang around anymore than was required. His parting word was that he would get my prescription drawn up so I could take it to the pharmacy before I left, this may take an hour or so as he had the rest of his patients to visit before he got back to his office.

In fact, it took four hours, bad planning by me as I had not ordered my lunch the day before; I thought I would be long gone by then.

The prescription arrived, Pat took me up to the pharmacy and we handed it in, it would be ready in about two hours, back to the ward and sat on the bed twiddling my thumbs. My saving grace was that Rhian had brought me in a tub of Rocky Road chocolates. Common sense told me that without lunch I would need some energy inside to ensure I didn't feel faint with the exploits ahead. I ate the lot, I hadn't eaten chocolate for about forty years; not something on my favourite wish list of food, boy did I feel sick after scoffing the whole tub.

Lee was going to be our taxi so Pat phoned him and said give it an hour and then come in, but grab a wheelchair at the exit.

It was about 4pm when I eventually left the ward for the last time, goodbyes had long been said, good lucks exchanged and everyone giving me that envious stare that I must have given departing patients over the last four weeks. A small wait at the pharmacy and then apologies that it had taken so long, but there was a lot to procure. Two month's supply of seven different tablets.

It was the strangest feeling being wheel-chaired through the hospital by your son, holding a very large bag of drugs. I had this feeling of total insecurity, I was actually going out into the real world in a wheelchair. I was sad and deliriously happy, all morning I had thought of this moment and I actually felt totally useless, even getting into the car was a massive struggle.

The trip home was uneventful but to me it was one of the greatest adventures I had been on in my life, just the small things like seeing a dog walking the streets, kids walking home from school, the inevitable queue at the roundabout at Shepherds Hill, the new Marks and Sparks petrol station on the A4; what prisoners must think after they have been incarcerated for years is mind blowing and how they would handle real life again just beggars belief.

And finally, we arrive home. Yep, there were tears in my eyes, adrenaline pumping, I would walk to the house, I didn't want the wheelchair and I made it to the lounge unaided.

I WAS HOME!

Chapter 29

Recovery

Our house is not the most user friendly for someone recovering from eight weeks in hospital. There are two flights of stairs between the bedroom and lounge, they are not big flights, nine steps each. It took me a week to actually do both flights without stopping, it took me two weeks before I could do the four flights to the garden door from the bedroom, a total of thirty-two steps in all. Progress was slow but I was determined I was going to go back to normality, I had grandchildren to play with and another one on the way.

By the end of the first month I could comfortably manage the stairs; I then concentrated on walking distances outside, not far but I gradually built it up over a six-week period and by then I was walking a mile a day. My greatest achievement was being able to walk down to the pigs. Leo had done a great job looking after them the whole time I was out of action, they actually looked as if they had lost weight. They recognised my voice and on the first visit came over to see me and ignored their food.

During my stay in the two hospitals, I had lost a considerable amount of weight – just over three stones – so feeding the pigs and carrying bales of straw were still a long way ahead in my recovery aim.

The grandkids were a great comfort over this period; it's amazing at such a young age they can recognise the condition of people. Then one day I heard Lola say to Ayla, 'We'd better stop playing now, gamps will be tired.'

Ayla said, 'Yes, let's read him a story.'

Yep, there were probably tears in my eyes.

I was feeling good, although the hospital regime of a 5.30am start did not wear off and in fact six months later I have taken to writing this book at 5.30am in the morning. The mornings are good for me, I now write, I feed the animals, two pigs, thirteen pheasants, and at least twelve ducks on a regular basis. Midday I'm fine but I still get very tired at night, the first month or so I was in bed asleep by 9pm, now at least I last till 10pm.

I have very slowly got back into work, this week I had my first meeting in London. I made it up there and back all on my own and felt a great sense of achievement. I did not sleep the night before, ridiculous when you consider I used to go to London for meetings nearly every day. I have started driving although I still have not as yet ventured out in the night to drive.

My concentration, or lack of, was one of the biggest surprises. When I came home everyone was saying, 'You timed that just right with the Rugby Autumn series starting.' But I could not watch more than twenty minutes without switching off. It has taken a long time for this concentration to return, I forced myself to read a book and to read articles in papers that would not normally interest me.

We had been invited to some old friends for dinner; there would be six of us there. I was worried that I would not be able to join in or contribute much to the conversation, but worst of all, listen to what other people were saying. This was a big step and thanks must go to Mick, Kaye Nigel and Maree, who broke me in gently. I lasted the evening and I don't think I was too boring; they may disagree but at least they were still awake when we left.

On the medical side, I took the memory drug for four weeks; two weeks I took it every night and then two weeks every other night. I saw no change in my memory of events both prior or post operation, however, I did suffer the most horrendous nightmares when I took the drug. They were tiring nightmares; I would wake exhausted. When I reduced the drug down to one every other night it was still the same, I had a nightmare every other night. The nightmares were never the same but they always had the same theme; I was trying to get somewhere and being thwarted every way I tried, but also meeting people on the way I had not seen for years.

I strongly recall I went through similar nightmares when I was in the medically induced coma – was I already on this drug in Mallorca?

The rest of the drugs were mainly vitamin B supplements, evidently I was deficient in this vitamin mainly because I was undernourished; could this be because I hadn't eaten for six weeks? I also took folic acid to maintain the stomach wall. The only drug that actually related to the operation was Bisoprolol; this was used to maintain my blood pressure at the correct level, just one tablet a day.

When I saw the GP for my first review, I mentioned the nightmares with the memory drug and the lack of anything positive from their consumption. I was surprised, he was not surprised and then surprised he took no notes to record these facts, he showed no interest at all. I asked about the vitamin B supplements and he said if they are working carry on taking them they are doing you no harm. I asked if they were working and he said yes, my blood tests showed this, but I hadn't had a blood test since hospital, let's just carry on taking them for the moment.

It was then that I asked about a blood test for the memory drug and he dropped the bombshell about no driving for six months.

Six months have now passed, I have seen the GP once more and he did not ask about the memory drug. He was happy with my blood pressure and my general appearance. I am still on the vitamin B tablets and the Bisoprolol. I see him again in six months' time.

Physically, I feel in good shape; I still get tired about 10pm but my body is still geared to the fact of waking up at 5.30am. Looks like this will continue to be my normal day.

Chapter 30

The End, Not Quite

Well that's about it, after six long months, two in hospitals, no lifting, no driving and certainly not any alcohol, I am back to normal or as normal as one gets. It's interesting that not once during this period have I ever felt depressed; determined but never depressed. The support I have had from Pat and the kids and the joy that the grandchildren have given has been immense; without them I would never have recovered in such a relatively short time.

To be fair to the staff in both hospitals and my GP, they have been superb. Although I would and have queried some of their decisions, it is a sign of their achievements that I was in a fit condition to disagree with some of their decisions – I hope they appreciate that fact when they read this book.

My main stumbling block was the repatriation and the hallucinations. On the repatriation, I was determined to find a member of the flight crew who was with me for the whole flight and responsible for chartering my state of health during the flight. I got lucky, very lucky and although we have not physically met we have spoken over the phone. He confirms everything I remembered and had detailed for the doctors back in the UK, the only point he could not confirm was the fact that I actually walked when I got off the plane. He said they were under so much pressure to turn the plane around before the airport shut that he lost sight of me, but he did know I left the plane on a gurney; but with no ambulance there he was not sure what then took place. Their priority was to get airborne as soon as physically possible.

For me it blew away the argument that the doctors kept coming back to: that I was in a confused state on arrival. His recollection was that I was lucid and we even had a joke about the rugby before the chaos commenced. This part of the episode I will have to leave to rest; was I ever given the memory drug to clear my mind on this, I will never know.

The more worrying thing for me was the hallucinations, no explanation was ever given to me by either hospital. These had all taken place in the build up to the fateful night of my admission to the Hospital De Llevant. Septicaemia seemed to be the main culprit, although when I have been carrying out my research, it would appear the hallucinations had taken place prior to septicaemia. Their reality still sticks in my mind vividly – I certainly don't need any drug to recall these. I will always question this point, but have reserved myself to the opinion that it will always remain a mystery, albeit a very scary mystery.

The presence of Mary, or shall we just call her the presence, I was aware of her in my youth and this was nothing to do with anything connected with the operation. I am not scared of her, I find it comforting to know there is someone there looking out for me, she certainly had her hands full on this occasion – I hope I don't have to disturb her again in the future.

I have included in the final pages of this part of the book an insight into a strangulated hernia. To me a hernia was a hernia, it was something that no end of men suffer with. I was not aware of the serious state of the body when the hernia becomes strangulated. The intestines are clamped together and start to rot almost immediately – in my case they had turned to pulp and a great deal of them had to be cut away. It also affected the bladder, again some of this had to be removed. The fatality rate of a strangulated hernia is high – combine this with septicaemia and double pneumonia, and I can now look back and realise why I only had hours to live and why the recovery was so doubtful – I was extremely lucky.

I have deliberately decided not to name the drugs that I was taking; a little knowledge can sometimes be very dangerous. The memory drug was for me a complete waste of time and after I had completed the course of tablets, no one showed a slight bit of interest in what I had to say about the effects that took place in my mind.

The support from the Memory Clinic, something the psychiatrist kept pushing, never materialised, I believe they have forgotten me. The Cognitive school followed suit.

I intend to visit Hospital De Llevant in Mallorca during the summer to thank them for their help; Pat can then show me the actual inside of the hospital without her giving me a 360-degree tour on her IPad.

Our return to Casa Bora will be interesting; will our feelings have changed for our idyllic holiday home?

Chapter 31

A Strangulated Hernia

Since my recovery, I have spent some considerable time researching a strangulated hernia and septicaemia. I did not understand why a hernia should be so life threatening; I have known lots of men who have suffered with a hernia and although painful and caused extreme discomfort it was never life threatening. The operation had always seemed quite quick and the recovery period a matter of days rather than months.

I spoke to various doctors, the British Hernia Centre and the NHS advice bureau, along with, out of necessity, my travel insurer plus my own personal health insurer. The results were quite frightening, hence the need I think for this information to be included in the book.

It would appear that the strangulated hernia kicked off a whole medical cocktail of problems which when combined became an extremely lethal dose that I was very lucky to survive. It was only during my research that I became aware of the skill and the determination of the medical team in Mallorca and the UK. Without them, I would never have written this book or in fact seen my family again.

I must admit I have plagiarized some of the copy from the various web sites and books on the subject; I am not clever or technical enough to provide exact details of the condition without reference to such sources as the British Hernia Centre, the NHS, and various doctors who have all contributed to the subject.

I think we should start at the beginning.

Is a strangulated hernia dangerous?

Yes, very and can be fatal.

At best they can be extremely painful and are classed as surgical emergencies. They require urgent medical attention. Unfortunately, the warning might come on very suddenly. The first thing that happens is acute pain. This becomes extremely severe and nothing can relieve the pain, the onset can be measured in minutes and creates an extremely frightening scenario for the patient.

An emergency operation for a groin hernia carries a substantial mortality risk; the risk is increased substantially if a bowel resection is involved.

A strangulated hernia occurs when a window of weakness opens in the abdominal wall allowing intestines to poke through the wall, commonly this intestine is the bowel. The window then clamps shut while the bowel is poking through it. When the window closes, it is in effect clamping shut on the intestine, which in turn shuts off the blood vessels inside the intestine. This results in dead intestine and when that happens it causes all kinds of poisons to be released into the blood stream, which in turn causes septicaemia and ultimately death. When septicaemia takes hold of the body it can become fatal within three days.

With this information I was beginning to realise what my body had gone through, although I never had the pain that so many physicians and surgeons see at the onslaught of a strangulated hernia.

I certainly had the vomiting; this was intense and I could not keep anything down. The fever grew as the poisons took hold and I was told my blood pressure decreased alarmingly. The symptoms were there but not the pain normally associated with the process.

My symptoms tended to indicate that septicaemia was taking hold and the doctors recognised that the situation could be fatal, hence the urgency for the operation and then the lengthy time recovering in both intensive care units in Mallorca and in the UK. The continual topping up of the anti-biotic drip, although being a pain during my recovery, was essential to control the poisons in my body and blood.

In my limited summary, a hernia is not always fatal and can be repaired relatively easy. However, if ignored it can build up to a life threatening situation, with the mortality rate being far higher if an emergency operation is required because of strangulation.

If you are in any doubt about that small annoying pain, contact your GP, don't do the male thing and hope it will just disappear.

I hope I have scared you, it certainly scared me with the research I undertook. Thankfully, through the expertise of the medical staff in both countries, I recovered. Don't become an addition to the percentage of the mortality rate – seek advice.

Chapter 32

Port of Christ; the return

October the 25th 2014. I left the Island, along with three doctors, a pilot and co-pilot. Pat's plane was a bit more crowded with an extra one hundred and thirty people flying with her, although she didn't feel any comfort in the numbers surrounding her. She actually saw my jet taxiing for take-off and was worried that she would be delayed and not get back to the UK in time to meet me at the next hospital. In hindsight she didn't have to worry, I was so heavily sedated that my head was really in the clouds.

Eight months had now passed and it was time to face my fears and return to the Island. The doctors both in Mallorca and the UK had done their jobs well and it was now up to me to manage my brain and sort out the mysteries that were still lurking in there.

The return to Mallorca was twofold; first to gauge my reaction to our Villa and the events that occurred there, and then to meet the team of doctors and nurses that operated on me and went through three weeks of hell while I was confined to intensive care. Pat had told me about the incidents where I had to be strapped to the bed and they had to call her to come in and try and pacify me; I still have scars on my wrist where I was struggling to free myself from the straps. Despite constant sedation, my mind was living a very traumatic time and four dreams or experiences still remain with me, eight months later. I was hoping for some explanations to finally put the events behind me, or at least come to terms with them.

It was only recently that I found out that the doctors had given me very little chance of returning to a normal life and a 50% return of body normality would be acceptable and anything above that would be a huge bonus. I'm glad I wasn't aware of this until recently but it made me far more determined to sort out what were hallucinations and what was reality; I didn't on my arrival on the Island realise how difficult this was going to be.

We arrived at the airport to be greeted by Juanjo, a guy that we had got to know over the last three years who ran a taxi business out of Cala D'Or. He walked with a limp from a hip operation eight years ago and driving a taxi all day was not the best occupation to help the hip recover – but this was a holiday Island and you either became a waiter or drove a taxi and made as much money as you can in a short period of the summer months to get you through the very quiet winter period.

At Palma airport, you have two exits and unfortunately he had chosen the wrong one; there is a 50/50 chance of getting the right one and on this occasion luck had failed him. We saw him ambling back to the exit we had chosen, waving like mad telling us to stay there. He kissed Pat first and then turned to me with both arms open and gave me a huge and prolonged hug, something I had now got used to after my initial reaction of awkwardness when people kept grabbing me and holding me.

He immediately grabbed the trolley off me and scolded me for lifting the bags off the conveyor belt. He also had a go at Pat saying the bags were too heavy, but she explained that I needed a whole new wardrobe as I had lost 25kgs and nothing fitted me anymore.

The journey to Cala D'Or was uneventful, Juanjo had upbeat holiday music on the radio which destroyed any conversation, but I was happy with that as I prepared myself for opening the door at Casa Bora and confronting... what?

We arrived at the Villa and he immediately jumped out, opened my door – not Pat's – and then proceeded to carry the bags up the stairs and placed them on the bed. He then proceeded to tell Pat that when he picked us up to leave the bags on the bed and he would take them off and put them in the car. Pidgin Spanish and English delayed his departure but I think both Pat and Juanjo had agreed on a plan for our return.

Chapter 33

So here we were eight months later, the events of that night Friday the 1st of October still clear in both our minds, but not exactly similar in our memories.

Pat busied herself with unpacking whilst I walked around the Villa just trying to picture how the events over those three long days unfolded. Nothing felt strange, nothing out of place, in fact at that moment in time I felt nothing. The sun was shining and it seemed idyllic, why was I so worried about coming back. At that moment it was too hard to explain, the next ten days would help with the explanation.

Pat finished the unpacking and we needed to go to the supermarket to get supplies – only the basics such as milk, water, bread, etc. The big shop would come later, with Pat having left in such a hurry there was nothing in the villa that we could use. I turned the boiler and central heating on, it all fired up and on our return we hope the musty smell would have disappeared thanks to the heating kicking in.

Just outside the supermarket is a bar/café. A lot of the locals meet there to put the worlds to right; the amount of time they are in there it would seem that the world is in a very bad state. The waiter acknowledged us, big smile and a welcoming hand shake; he didn't hug me, which I found re-assuring. Pat ordered a cup of coffee and I ordered a beer. Nothing strange in that, but a huge moment for me. This was going to be the first beer I had had since the September 2014, nearly nine months. I enjoyed it but did not order another – one step at a time.

Essentials bought and back to the Villa, the first big test for me was to come. Watching the TV sat on the sofa, this was where it all began, that first prod in the back which I dismissed so lightly as a wayward spring. I was apprehensive and just felt plain awkward the whole evening. I was just waiting for some slight movement or feeling coming from the sofa, nothing happened but I could not really relax.

Time for bed and I insisted that I sleep in the spare bedroom on my own, exactly replicating the situation back in October. Pat asked did I want her to check the wardrobes and even tuck me in and turn the light off – I told her I had to handle this and just let me get on with it. I realised after that I was pretty abrupt and did apologise the next day.

One thing that fascinated me was the fact that despite all the hallucinations, the presence of bodies in the bedroom and Villa, the extreme vomiting, this alone should have been terrifying as it was like a scene from the exorcist with green puke running down the bathroom walls, I was never actually scared. There was no feeling of fear and in fact, I remember telling some of the life forms that I was just plain bored of their antics.

I lay in bed, in the dark just waiting, waiting for what I don't know; a sound, a poke in the back, anything that I had been subjected to previously, but nothing came, unfortunately, not even sleep.

I got up at about 5am, fed up of just lying there. It was still dark but I wanted to go for a walk just to clear my mind. I walked to the old fort and sat on the rocks overlooking the Med; the sea was pretty rough but the crashing of the waves on the rocks below me seemed to have a very therapeutic calming effect as I processed the non-events of the night in my head.

The sun rose and I walked back to the village to get some croissants for breakfast and pick up the paper. The women in the shop was genuinely pleased to see me. Yes, she gave me a big hug, we talked football, but she kept staring at me and then holding my hand. Again, pigeon English and Spanish prevailed but it would appear she was shocked by the amount of weight I had lost, so much so that she either forgot to charge me for the croissant or felt she was helping me to get back to a fuller figure as soon as possible.

Got back to the Villa, and Pat's first question was where had I been. She was naturally worried and I hadn't taken my phone or left a note. Again, another apology but I hadn't thought about those things at the time.

The one main thing that had changed since the operation was my sleeping patterns and the little amount of sleep I needed plus the dreams that would occur every night.

I regularly awoke between 5.30am and 6am, something that I had got used to in the hospitals and could not shake the habit on my return to normal existence. The other thing was that by 10.30pm I am ready for bed and go off to sleep immediately. I always and still do sleep solidly until 2am after that it's just hit and miss.

I made sure for the rest of the time on the Island I took my phone with me each morning, just in case Pat needed me.

Chapter 34

Cala D'Or is a relatively small place and it became quite apparent over the next couple of days that news of my illness had spread around the village quite quickly back in October. I was constantly being stopped and hugged and asked about my health and then hugged again.

When I popped down to the baguette shop to pick up lunch, it was like the prodigal son had returned; more hand shaking, lots of hugging and again they didn't charge me. Forget the favourable exchange rate, this illness was suddenly starting to have its benefits.

The second night we decided to have a BBQ; again chicken legs the size of cows and veg to die for, followed by a cheeky chocolate ice lolly. Unfortunately, my new found wealth situation didn't extend to the butchers and they charged me the going rate, didn't even get a hug.

After the BBQ, the night followed the same course as the previous; me feeling edgy on the sofa, Pat continually asking if I was all right and then attempting to sleep alone again in the spare bedroom.

The good thing was I did manage some sleep and felt a lot better in the morning, but it felt as if I was continually waiting for something to touch me or start tapping in the wardrobe.

I went for a walk early and bumped into our lawyer walking her dog. Again some big hugs, starting to get relaxed with the situation and I'm sure I made the first move that morning. We walked down around the marina on what was a beautiful sunny morning. Talk was mostly about the op, I have tended to leave out the hallucination side of events, it's hard to explain in English, let alone Spanish. It was quite a jovial chat, with Marion having a very good sense of humour for a lawyer, but as we neared the end of the marina she said I should really consider a Spanish will urgently, because if there is not one in place the Spanish Government can grab the villa and take it into their possession. I agreed I would pop down to her office that afternoon to make an appointment. I carried on my walk past the garage and proceeded along the main highway towards Cala Serena.

The footpath was quite good and I made good progress with some all-out power walking. I had not been along this route before but it was well signposted and said Cala Serena was 6km away. The footpath dis-appeared after about another 1km and it became very rural. I stopped when I saw this small holding that appeared to have some pigs just lying there soaking up the morning sun. The pigs were quite small, nothing like the two I've got at home but I counted five of them.

Something caught my eye and further down the track there were some chickens, but I also caught a flash of blue through a forest of prickly pear bushes. I approached the stone wall and the area was securely fenced, along with an inner fence which would form a second barrier for someone when they went into feed the chickens. It looked very familiar and I remember saying to myself last time I saw such a setup, what a clever idea and something I should do with mine at home.

It was then that I saw the peacocks, two of them, strikingly blue with the sun shining on their extended feathers.

I stood still and it all came back to me; this was a major part of my hallucination period. I had woken up on the Thursday morning, back in October, early, it was still dark and I had heard something on the vacant land next to Casa Bora. I had ventured out just with a pair of shorts on and there, next door, someone had fenced off the land with a structure exactly the same as I was standing in front of now and inside were chickens, two peacocks, blue, two ponies, brown and white, and something else that was not coming back into my head.

This was exactly my hallucination, I just stood there gob smacked, too much going through my head, how had I seen this in such exact detail? I had never been down here before, walking or driving, this was unbelievable. I couldn't move, I was frozen to the spot, I remembered everything about the hallucination and here it was, right in front of me. I could feel my heart pumping and my head was buzzing, how, how, how?

I wanted to do so much, phone Pat, no phone, take a picture, no phone, balls balls balls!!! I'm about 4km from the villa, fifteen-minute walk, do I leave and get the phone, will the whole scene di-appear again? I touch the fence, I touch the wall, it's all solid. I watch the chickens, I watch the peacocks, it's all there in front of me. Wait, no ponies, I look everywhere, no ponies, no ponies.

I move sideways looking everywhere for the ponies. The chickens and peacocks follow me, they want feeding. Nothing around, it's all barren, more prickly pear bushes but nothing else. Again, I keep touching the fence, the wall, it's all real, it's solid, it's real, no ponies, no ponies…

My mind is going into overdrive. I'll walk back to the villa, get the phone, tell Pat, bring her back with me. No wait, this is what happened in the hallucination, when I rang the doorbell because I had forgotten the keys, Pat came to the door and I grabbed her and dragged her to the land next door and it had all disappeared – I couldn't let it happen again. Shit, was I going mad again? Fuck, fuck, fuck!

I started to walk back to the villa, everything going through my mind; not again please, not again.

I stopped and I went back. It was still there, I touched everything, solid, why, what, I just didn't know, this was not supposed to happen, this was not supposed to happen.

Walk, walk, do something. I walked to Cala Serena, illogical. I sat down on the beach and just looked at the sea, waves pounding inside and outside my head. What had I just seen, did I see it, did I fucking see it?

Peacocks, do they exist in Mallorca? Have I ever seen any in all the years we have been coming? No, had I seen these, are they part of my brain that won't let go? Touch the sand, it's real. Take off my crocs, stand in the sea, it's bloody cold but it's real. Splash water on my face, shit that's cold, it's real.

DO SOMETHING.

Chapter 35

Two people invade my space, 'Hola, sprechen se Deutsch?'

'Nien, English.'

'Do you know where the bakery is?'

'The bakery, this is the beach.'

'Ya but is the bakery nearby?'

'No, there is one in Cala d'Or.'

'Danke.'

Off they go, heading in the wrong direction. 'Hold on, Cala d'Or is over there, about 8kms away'

'Danke.'

'Do you have the time?'

'It's 8am.'

'Thank You, Addios.'

Right Michael, walk back, slowly, composed, let's see the birds again, let's make sure they are real, let's think about this.

The hallucination is at the forefront of my mind, everything I've seen this morning; it was in the hallucination, but no ponies, everything else, the wall, the fencing, the chickens, the peacocks. The peacocks, I have never seen peacocks on the Island before, why does someone keep peacocks, can you eat them, can you cook their eggs, what use are they? What use am I, just a piece of wasted flesh mumbling along a country road, not really believing what I am seeing or doing. 8am, I've been out for two hours, got to tell Pat, got to get back, short cut. No, I've got to see the birds again, the fence, the wall.

It takes me about ten minutes and I am in front of the wall. They are all there; again I touch everything solid, the chickens are in front of me, they still want feeding, just like all chickens, the peacocks are strutting around in the back, doing nothing in particular but looking resplendent.

It's real, it's definitely bloody real, it exists, it's there, it's definitely there, I'm not bloody mad.

I walk to the side of the compound and I now notice there are different sections. Some parts are growing veg, some have got flowers in, and then there are the pigs. It's like a set of allotments all sectioned off with stone walls, hand built stone walls, no cement all stones laid on top of each other. The chickens have the fencing on top of the walls, with an inner fence; the pigs have barbed wire on top of the walls and the vegetable gardens just have ordinary straight wire on the top of the walls – it's all really well done and spaced out. The pigs house is four huge bails of straw, they must weigh a ton each and it works well, and then I see behind the straw house – two fucking ponies, brown and white. Fuck me, I am fucking mad.

Chapter 36

I walk back to the Villa, go inside, have a drink of water and Pat says, 'Are you alright?'

'Yep fine.'

I go outside and lay on the sun bed. I lay there most of the morning, it's a beautiful day. Pat's worried I am so quiet, I've got nothing to say, no, re-phrase, I don't know what to say. I tell her about meeting Marion down by the marina, I tell her we need to go down and make an appointment with her to make a will. I tell her that I walked to Cala Serena, I tell her about the Germans wanting the bakery, I tell her everything but nothing about the chickens, the peacocks, the ponies.

We walk down to Marion's, she sees us straight away, we go through the will and she phones the notary in Felixitna, the will has to be signed in his presence. Arrangements are made for Monday, 9.30am; Tuesday we are going up to Porto Cristo to meet the doctors and their teams, must remember to get a car organised.

Come out of Marion's and go down to the Plaza. Pat has a coffee, I have a beer, don't remember drinking it. Still not said a thing about my morning, don't know how to start, what effect will it have on Pat. She thought the worst is behind us, do I tell her? I must tell her, maybe not now, maybe never. No, I must tell her, but not now.

Chapter 37

I wanted the night to pass quickly, dinner was a quiet affair, lucky we went to Portofina, great fish, catch of the day was John Dory, beautiful in onions. The staff made a big fuss of us and kept the conversation going all night, I refused a nightcap and just walked home.

Sleep was hard to come by; I just wanted to get up and go walking, I needed to see the farm again – the images were in my head all through the night, nothing shifting them, it couldn't really be right. Did I walk there on the night that they stick in my mind, the night the fever was at its highest, was it physically possible? How would I have done it in the dark, I needed to check nearest street lights. So many questions and no answers.

I was clearly spooked and nothing was making sense, there is only so much that google can help you with.

Left the villa at 6am, walked slowly to see how long it would take if I had managed to walk there that fateful night. twenty-five minutes it took, no street lights within a kilometre, no way could I have made it in the dark and certainly no chance of seeing anything. Would the chickens be out anyway? At home they would be tucked up in their hut until dawn.

They were all there; peacocks, chickens and the two ponies. Again, constant touching of the fence and wall, it was still solid. I turned away and walked back, still slowly, still took twenty-five minutes.

Carried on walking down to the sea, sat on the rocks at Cala Gran beach and just tried to analyse what I had in my mind.

The farm existed, that I was pretty sure of.

The animals were there and they were the ones I saw in my hallucination.

Was it an hallucination, big question mark.

Could I have walked there in the dark, totally screwed out of my mind? And if I did manage it, could I have seen anything in the dark, we definitely did not have a torch in the Villa.

How and when do I tell Pat, do I tell Pat?

'Hello Stranger, didn't know you were back on the Island. So you didn't die then, must have been close from what I hear.'

It was Mick from the Lost Sock, a laundrette on the outskirts of the village, I had used it for the last couple of years, kept my clothes down there whenever we returned to the UK, always washed and ironed ready for me to pick up when we returned to Cala d'Or.

'Bloody hell you've lost weight; no wonder you didn't bring your clothes in when you went back to the UK.'

I explained to him about the airlift back and carried on about the whole chain of events, not mentioning my recent discovery. We sat there for well over an hour, throwing sticks in the water for his big old dog Reggie, yep, named after the Krays. He wanted to know all the gory details about the op, didn't seem so interested in the recovery, pretty animated about the private jet back and then the subject changed to what a shit season he had last year and things needed to recover quickly this year for him to survive.

'Right, I'm off, need to open up, get the machines going, pop in for a beer sometime,' not an offer you get from your usual laundrette.

'Hold on I'll come with you,' my train of thought had totally gone, so no point hanging around contemplating the farm and occupants, I needed a swim to clear my head.

The next three days passed quite quickly. Only tried one morning walk in with a visit to the farm; still there, still solid to touch, still hadn't told Pat, but I had come up with a plan to tell her Monday. Visited the notary, he witnessed the wills, saw we were both born in Cardiff and then proceeded to talk about Cardiff Castle for twenty minutes; thankfully, we were not paying him by the hour.

Bite to eat on the way back in to Porto Petro, sat on the harbour side eating sardines and watching the world go by. Pat asked if I was nervous about the visit to the Hospital the next day. I said I was, but also excited. She said her stomach was churning over and wasn't sure how she was going to handle it, worried that they wouldn't recognise us or her. I assured her that they wouldn't have agreed to see us if that was the case.

Had a walk around the port and went over to the rocks and just sat there catching some rays, was this the time to tell her? But failed miserably, didn't want to spoil what was a very pleasant afternoon.

Chapter 38

Tuesday 19th May 2015, the day had finally come around for my return to the Hospital De Levant, Porto Cristo, or as the locals call it, Port of Christ due to the Christian conquest of the Island back in 1260AD when they arrived at the port believing it was Palma and brought a huge cross of Jesus on land and erected it at the port.

I was so itching to get there; I had showered, shaved and eaten breakfast before 6am and I don't think I sat down once the whole time, just pacing around waiting for us to leave. Pat surprised me and then totally blew me away when she told me the route to take.

She said her and Rhian had found a short cut that saved about 15kms and cut the journey down by about twenty minutes; when she told me the way I immediately realised it took us right past the farm.

My brain quickly scrambled this information and this would be the opportunity to tell her about my findings, we would drive past the farm and see if she saw it, again on the way back I would drive past it and then turn around at the roundabout and drive back to it and tell her all about it. I wanted to see if there was any recognition from her as we drove past it, would this somehow answer the questions I had in my head? Not sure, but the day had certainly got off to an exciting start.

As we set off, she suddenly said, 'I am so nervous, I just don't know what we will find, I feel sick in my stomach.' We drove past the farm, I felt myself slowing down, nothing from Pat in any shape or form. In all honesty, I glanced quickly but you just cannot see anything from the road.

The journey took twenty minutes; we had allowed an hour. Pat had said it was an hour but with the short cut it would be about forty minutes. A bit way out on the timing but I didn't care – we were there.

I had a leather covered book that I had been using since my recovery, making notes of everything I remembered, all the questions I had and all the mysteries that could not be explained. As could be expected, the last few pages were completely devoted to the farm.

The two main things I had identified for the hospital visit was the church in the centre of Porto Cristo and the Italian General Major, who was in overall charge of the hospital. Pat had been pretty dismissive of both, she had never seen this Italian, who from my description was six feet, four inches, built like a rugby player and extremely smart and handsome, always wore a check shirt with jeans and loafers. I had met him before in Hong Kong and we talked most days and on the other point, the church was impossible to see from my window and the fact that I could not get out of bed to get to the window was another major point that blew this fact away.

In the leather book I had detailed the description of the Church clock tower which I had seen in my mind and the curvature of the Church something I found hard to explain, but it was from either the front or back of the Church and it was a curved wall embracing the main tower and raising up about 30ft. It was as if the wall was holding the tower and protecting it, as I say, hard to explain but I had clearly seen it in my mind, the mind that at the time was heavily sedated.

We pulled off the ring road roundabout and Pat directed me to the car park. I didn't need directions I knew exactly where it was; I couldn't have, I had never approached the hospital from the car park, the ambulance had taken me around the back to A & E and on my departure I left through the same entrance, never once did I go to the car park.

But there we were, parked up on a piece of derelict land that I distinctly remember, I parked in front of an old fishing boat that had just been dumped there many years ago, the top half was blue, the bottom half was white. I don't remember having made a note of the boat before, either in my book or in my mind, but the colour blue was important to me in some way, I didn't know why.

Pat was on the phone to her friend Jill, lots of 'oohs' and 'aahs' and congratulations, etc. I had no time for that, I needed to get out and walk around, I was here and I needed to absorb everything. I don't know how long Pat was on the phone and I know that she told me something when she got out of the car, but I had no time for anything that detracted from what was going through my mind and body. I was shaking from the inside out and it was as if my brain was in overdrive, thousands of things passing through it, some being recognised and noted, some just being dismissed.

The first thing I saw and was immediately drawn to was the clock tower; it was exactly as I remember it, the clock tower I had or could never have seen. I turned to face the hospital, I recognised my room immediately, how could I have seen the tower, I couldn't but I had, how?

I paced the car park; in the line of sight from my room was a tree blocking the view of the tower or so I thought. The more I moved around, I realised the tree blocked the line of sight for every other room, but not from mine, my room was the only possible room that you could see the tower from.

Pat caught up with me at the entrance gates, I pointed to the room and said that was where I was. She said, 'No, it was not, don't be so stupid, that's not the room; I will show you as we walk around where yours was.'

I insisted that was the room, I pointed out the room on the other side of the U-shaped building and said I looked at that all day, it was totally blocked off with no windows – I always thought that's where the dead bodies go, hence no windows.

Pat was having none of this and said, 'I will show you now your room.' I was adamant that was the room. We walked to the right of the building that took us around to the back and A & E. Pat stopped at the corner of the building and said, 'I think you're right, I've just got my bearings and that is your room.'

I walked back and stood in front of the gates looking at the room, then turning around looking at the clock tower, it was all there in my brain, the boat – why was the colour so important, nothing registering, nothing.

Chapter 39

Around at the A & E entrance I remembered little except for the doors with their logo on and the fact that they were automatic, I remember being wheeled in through them. Reception looked nothing like I remembered it, but it was afterwards while we were leaving that I mentioned that to Pat and she said it had all been re-modelled with new walls in place.

The blonde receptionist, who I later found out was called Maria, was busy with a customer. As soon as she saw Pat, she moved the customer on to her assistant. She came around the counter and gave Pat the biggest hug and kisses possible, tears on both faces while I stood there like a spare part. Pat then introduced me and Maria nearly smothered me with her joy, she was the one that booked me in and was our first contact with the hospital. It was all a very moving moment for us all and the other receptionist and customer just looked and kept smiling, it was pretty emotional.

Loads of questions asked, loads answered on both sides and it was such a joy to talk to someone who knew what we had gone through.

Pat showed me the actual area I was kept in prior to going up to the operation theatre. I remembered it all, including where Pat made the call to the HSBC after receiving the information from AXA that I was not covered on their policy. A most frightening moment, something that I suppose went over my head, but Pat had to deal with it, an incredibly stressful moment and one she will always remember. Thank God for HSBC, true life savers.

After Maria calmed down, she said she would phone the doctors and let them know we were here; they were actually in the Intensive Care Ward and did we want to go up and wait outside until they were free.

We went through the door to the lift, this was all new to me, I didn't remember any of this but then it suddenly hit me; all the doors and bannisters were blue, the same blue that I saw on the boat, that was what had triggered my memory. Coming out of the lift, the blue was everywhere, at least one bit of madness explained.

Pat showed me where I was taken for examination. Nothing to really remember there – white room, a very high tech bed, instruments hanging from the gantry above, very bright. I then saw the operating theatre, a lot more memories there, a lot bigger than the holding room, not so bright and full of machines; again, one very big high tech bed.

We then waited outside the door (blue) to the intensive care ward, adrenaline was now pumping so much I could feel that I was getting light headed. A nurse came around the corner from the direction we had just come from, she gave me the biggest smile and nearly shouted out, 'Michael, you look so well, I will get Dr Sospedra.' With that a small blonde haired nurse came out of the door from Intensive Care, smiling laughing and immediately came over and gave me a big hug, and then another one. Her English was not good, always remember that, but she had held my hand so often and it seemed the natural thing to do to hold both hers. Not much conversation but just being there together, laughing and smiling, hugging, it didn't need words.

The door opened again and out came the doctor and nurse who had gone to get him. He came over to Pat, no handshakes, just straight into hugs, big hugs. Pat blubbed straight away, a lot of moistness in the doctor's eyes; then the doctor turned to me and I went to shake his hand; he was having none of that and grabbed me and hugged me so tight I think he thought he was performing the Heimlich manoeuvre. I became aware that the nurse was still holding my hand, awkward.

I realised no words had been spoken; we were all just content to smile, laugh and hug. I can't describe it better than that but it was a pure show of enjoyment.

The Doctor broke the ice, said I was looking superb, I looked so well, we laughed about a few things, mainly how bad I had looked. He wanted to know how much I remembered because I was so heavily sedated the whole time, they had expected me to be with them for three days max, not three weeks, and they had to use major sedation the whole time. Told him what I remembered, Pat told him about my treatment back in the UK and then I asked him about the one question that was very important to me: the Italian General Major of the hospital, who was he, where was he? I could not find him on their website, nothing about him. I recall seeing him every day and in fact, he would come in sometimes with the doctor.

The Doctor answered first and said there was no one there from Italy, the CEO was Gabriel Adrover, Spanish. Neither nurse knew who I was talking about despite me describing him in detail.

Hard to take this in, but again the door opened and another two staff arrived; one a very pretty blonde haired Doctor, who I had christened Miss Balearics 2014, and a male nurse Christian, who wore his hair in a ponytail.

The blonde doctor hugged me continually, we kept grabbing each other and just holding each other; sounds pervy, but she was probably the one who spent the most time with me and she kept saying Michael, Michael, Michael. She patted my stomach, where had it gone we laughed, we all laughed. The corridor was quite packed now with seven of us all occupying the space, but it was one hell of a happy place.

I asked them about the mystery Italian but again a total blank, Christian said he went to Italy for his holidays and was not with me the last week I was on the ward, was there a tie up there in my mind, I don't think so. This Italian General Major will always exist in my mind.

All too soon our meeting had to come to an end, they were all working and had to get back to their duties. It was strange, we were all reluctant to pull apart; what Pat and I thought could have been a very awkward meeting turned out to be one hell of an event. We both actually think that the doctor and his team were so happy to see us that it was one of those genuine and joyous moments in your life you always remember – we certainly will.

Big disappointment: we couldn't go onto the ward but it was not really unexpected; this was intensive care and patients could not really be disturbed just because the circus had come to town.

Farewells said, last hugs, handshakes, a big thank you to them all for saving my life and we were alone, back down the corridor, last look at the operating theatre and the holding room and we were at reception.

Chapter 40

Maria came from behind the counter, still more hugs and smiles, we thanked her for her help, one final hug and we were outside.

I walked around a bit before we went back to the car and the hospital blue boat. We dropped off Pat's bag and then proceeded to walk down to the port. Pat wanted to show me her daily route and she wanted to go back to the Hotel Felip, which looked after her so well, and I wanted to offer my thanks to them at the same time.

The area to start with was a bit dodgy and I could see why she didn't want to walk down there on her own in the dark. Back in October last year with the tourists gone and the dark early nights I could imagine it becoming quite intimidating.

I was quite amazed how complicated the one-way system was even just walking, you never knew where the cars were coming from.

We got to the road that took us to the church and started to walk up it. The pavements were very small and most of the time you had to walk in the road with the occasional car coming up behind you.

Pat saw the church first and commented on the window slots in the tower and how dangerous they could be if a small child was climbing the stairs. It was only as we got closer that she could see railings through the slots to prevent this. She did say that she had not noticed this before when she had seen it, but then again her head was in a very distressed state.

They were trimming the trees in the church garden, quite dramatically, so much so that there were no branches left. There were eight trees in total, all very neatly laid out looking like soldiers on guard; in fact, the whole church looked more like a castle than a church – it did not give you that feeling of warmth and it appeared to be built more for defence than comfort.

Pat went to the right of the church but I carried on. Pat shouted to say, 'You can't go that way, they've blocked the road because of all the cut branches.' I ignored her and she followed, I walked past the barriers and the branches and chipper and there in front of me was the curvature of the wall that I had seen in my mind; it was exactly as I had seen it, exactly.

The hairs on the back of my neck were standing up and a very strange tickle was going through my body, it was as if an electric current was tingling my whole nervous system.

It was there, it was real, the curved wall a bit more than thirty feet high but holding the clock tower as if to offer it protection. I had to touch it, it was real, it was definitely bloody real.

Pat asked was I alright; I was just standing there staring, an awful lot going through my mind, how is this real, how is the Italian not, and yet the farm is. No answers, just questions.

She held my hand and we walked back around the barriers and branches and went down the side of the Church around to the front. It actually looked quite normal and in fact quite imposing as it was set back from the road and there were about twenty steps leading down to the road. I would imagine a beautiful place to take pictures for a wedding.

Pat said, 'Shall we go inside?'

Something made me immediately say, 'No, I didn't want to.'

She said, 'We might as well now that we are here.' But again something made me say no, more determined this time.

Can't explain that but I definitely did not want to go inside, still didn't when we came back after lunch.

We carried on and walked down to the Hotel, this was a far busier area with loads of quaint looking shops, busy sidewalks and had a very holiday mood about the place.

The hotel was on the main front overlooking the beach, the main road through Porto Cristo ran in front of the hotel and formed a barrier between the hotel and the beach. The hotel had a balcony area on the front where people were sitting down enjoying a drink whilst they watched the world go by. I was amazed how many big coaches were passing by only a few feet away. From a very dodgy area by the hotel, the port had suddenly come alive and it felt as if everyone was enjoying themselves in the bright midday sun.

I realised we had stopped on the steps of the hotel and there was an official looking women talking to a couple of people who I assumed were customers. She seemed anxious to turn around and see us, of course it was the Manageress that Pat had told me about, bit of slow thinking on my part.

The customers walked over to a table and sat down, the women stood there just smiling. Pat went to say, 'Do you remember me?' but by that time the women had hugged her and cut her words short.

I couldn't see if Pat was blubbing because she had her head buried into the Manageress's shoulder; I suspected she was, again I was bit of a spare part standing on the entrance steps in the way of everyone whilst these two women were embracing in front of me.

Pat introduced me and we moved to one side, lots of hand shaking, questions and again she hugged me. The sheer welcome we had had all morning was overpowering and gave you a great sense of love – something you don't often experience from people you hardly know, or does three weeks of distressed life count as a lifetime friendship?

We chatted and I thanked her profusely for looking after Pat; she kept saying how well I looked and she would never have imagined I had been ill. We ordered some drinks and sat down on the balcony, the Manageress had to go off to attend a constant stream of customers. This was a very busy place.

Drinks arrived, Pat didn't know the waiter, but in a holiday place like this, I would have thought the staff turnover was extremely high. It was amusing how the waiters had to carry drinks across the road to the tables on the promenade side, dodging buses and cars, with their trays acting as shields.

Pat had told me about an incident where she and Rhian were sat on the promenade and the waiter was coming across with their drinks, a car came around the tight corner, a quick flick of the waiter's hips to avoid it and the drinks and tray went everywhere.

The hotel itself was nothing like I had imagined, it had the elegance of a historic French hotel inside; the dark wood, the chrome, the old drink dispensers, it really was very nice. I needed a pee so on my trip to the loo I explored the dining room and stumbled into the kitchen area by mistake.

I was so impressed that Lee and Rhian had stumbled on such a perfect place to look after Pat during the hospital stay.

Returning from the loo, I stopped and talked to the Manageress; she was still so bubbly and she went to shake my hand for the kind thanks that I had given her, lucky I had washed them, but instead she grabbed me and hugged me again.

Time to move on and we walked down the promenade and along the beach. Pat wanted to show me where she had her down time when not visiting me. Although the sun was shining and people were enjoying themselves it was quite sad when she said she would sit there overlooking the sea, just crying and not being able to stop; lucky as she said no one was around at that time of the year.

We carried on walking over to a cave in the rocks where she wanted to show me the history of Porto Cristo. She had told me about this quite a lot when I was drugged up but I still remembered that there was a video constantly playing in the cave giving all the historic facts. Unfortunately, the video had gone and the cave had bars across it, big disappointment.

We walked back and in front of the hotel we stopped and Pat showed me the room she had overlooking the sea; she got a bit emotional, the old bottom lip started to quiver and we moved on.

We stopped for lunch in a nice restaurant in a quieter bit of the port, we discussed what had happened that morning and at the hotel, and we both had such a warm feeling inside that I'm sure anyone looking at us could see a glow emanating from our bodies.

Chapter 41

We headed back to the hospital to pick up the car, I needed to see the church again. We approached it by the same road, the barriers had gone and the branches cleared up, I hadn't noticed before that it was actually pedestrianised. At the curved wall I turned left and walked along the street for about fifty yards. I stopped and turned around, Pat looking at me quizzically; 'This is how I remember it perfectly, this is where I saw it from.'

I couldn't explain the exact moment, but I knew I had been there, as Pat said, 'Absolutely impossible.'

That previous feeling I had when I first saw the curved wall, the electric charge passing through my body had gone, I felt contentment, I was at ease with my thoughts, I had been here.

How, when, why, I will probably never know, there's no way the ambulance would have come down here and Pat was with me when they brought me to the hospital. There's no way I could have seen it from the hospital, I couldn't walk, so that was out, as Pat said, absolutely impossible.

We carried on walking, the street was entirely straight, we turned left about half a mile along and I looked back. The definition of the curved wall had blended into one, the only thing I was certain about was I had seen it before, somehow.

I started the car, stopped in front of the hospital entrance and looked up at my room. I said goodbye in my mind, drove to the end of the street and turned left to get onto the ring road. I stopped – I suddenly realised I had seen Christian the male nurse walking his dog down this street. I was looking down at him, I didn't tell Pat enough is enough, but I wrote it in my book as soon as I could.

Onto the ring road and not thinking straight I took the wrong turning, didn't realise and ended up on the way to Manacor. By the time we both realised we were about 10kms from Manacor; too late to turn back, so we drove around the edge of the town and let the good old homing system find us a way back.

It probably put about another thirty minutes on the journey but it wasn't surprising that my mind was all over the place, I shouldn't have driven, I was punch drunk, lucky the roads were quiet.

By the time we got back on the right road I was determined to finish the day off – I was going to show Pat the farm.

I slowed down as we approached it and then drove past and went down to the next roundabout, turned around and came back. Pat was confused and asked what I was doing. I pulled over on the side of the road and asked her to get out and follow me.

We crossed the road and headed towards the clump of prickly pear bushes. 'Mike what are you doing? You're scaring me.'

'Just follow me, I'll show you.'

I went to the left of the bushes and said look. There was the farm in front of her, the wall, the fence, the chickens, two peacocks, no damn ponies.

Pat looked at me and said, 'Oh my God, I should have believed you, I am so sorry.'

I touched the wall; it was solid. We drove back to the Villa in silence.

Chapter 42

Two hundred years ago I would have been burnt at the stake as a witch, lucky for me that practice has now stopped.

I cannot explain what has taken place in my mind, how I have seen things I could not possibly have seen. There are other minor events that took place that, again, I have no explanation for and I have come to the conclusion that I never will have an answer to so many things that have happened in this book.

The one thing I can say with certainty is that my memory of events, the places, the people involved are clear in my mind, the clarity of all this is very strong, even when I was in the drug induced coma.

It will never go away, I need to handle it and come to terms with the fact that I will never know.

Hallucinations or Reality? Your choice, but for me my mind is already made up.

EVERY DAY
IS A FRESH
BEGINNING

EVERY DAY
IS A FRESH
BEGINNING

Meaningful
Poems
for
Life

Chosen by
AOIBHÍN GARRIHY

eriu

First published in the UK in 2022 by Eriu
An imprint of Bonnier Books UK
5th Floor, HYLO,
103–105 Bunhill Row
London, EC1Y 8LZ

The acknowledgments on pages 173–75 constitute an extension
of this copyright page

Twitter – @eriu_books
Instagram – @eriubooks

A CIP catalogue record for this book is available from the British Library.

Hardback ISBN: 978-1-80418-081-5
Paperback ISBN: 978-1-80418-131-7
eBook ISBN: 978-1-80418-171-3

Also available as an ebook and an audiobook

1 3 5 7 9 10 8 6 4 2

Typeset in Bodoni by Envy Design Ltd
Printed and bound in Great Britain by Clays Ltd, Elcograf S.p.A.

www.bonnierbooks.co.uk

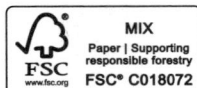

MIX
Paper | Supporting
responsible forestry
FSC
www.fsc.org
FSC® C018072

For Mom and Dad with all my love x

Contents

Introduction

POETRY IS LANGUAGE AT ITS MOST DISTILLED
AND MOST POWERFUL

Rita Dove

Poetry has always been a constant in my life.
During the milestones, the big moments, poetry
seemed to mark each and every one. But it was also
there in the quieter times, a form of solace and a path
to meditation, bringing me comfort and inspiration
when I needed it most. It always featured to such a
degree that I almost took it for granted and forgot the
power it holds for me.

It took a few turbulent years and a global pandemic
for me to realise how much I truly valued the healing
power of words. I found myself turning to poetry more
and more when I felt confused, angry, overwhelmed,

sad but also elated, overjoyed and totally in love. I was drawn to the words of others and sometimes even felt compelled to write myself, however simply.

Perhaps poetry requires you to be in a certain headspace. Lockdown gave us that time, that headspace and the spark was reignited for me and so many others, it seems.

In 2020 I took to my wardrobe (it was the closest thing to a sound recording booth!) and began to read, recite, record and share some poems that had a deep meaning for me, and it was possibly my biggest awakening over the past few years. I recently heard Ethan Hawke speak about poetry and art and how in our hour of need, it's no longer a luxury; it's sustenance. We need it. This was certainly true for me.

Now, I keep my poetry books by my bed and at the end of the day, depending on my mood or what's going on that day, I scan those books for that sustenance, a poem, some healing words to help me process a particular emotion or feeling. That for me is therapy.

My love for poetry began with my dad. He left school at sixteen but that didn't stop his poetic flair – a great man to put pen to paper should the mood take him. He wrote four rhyming stanzas titled 'Aoibhín O Aoibhín' on the back of a cigarette box while I was watching from the buggy on a lazy sunny afternoon! The poem detailed the delightful nappy-changing cycle and it still hangs proudly in Mom and Dad's

downstairs loo. It didn't make the final cut for this anthology, needless to say, but I'm delighted one of his more recent works does!

I think for most of us, our relationship with poetry began with our teachers. I was lucky enough to have wonderful teachers who instilled a love and appetite for poems and poetry recitation in me from a very early age. I remember learning and reciting my very first poem at the school *feis*, 'Queen Bee' by Mary K. Robinson. I still remember every line:

When I was in the garden,
I saw a great Queen Bee:
She was the very largest one
That I did ever see.
She wore a shiny helmet
And a lovely velvet gown,
But I was rather sad, because
She didn't wear a crown!

In second class I had a very special teacher, Miss Susan Ryan. One of those teachers who leaves a lasting impression on you, forever etched in your heart. I was besotted with her. We all were. She was larger than life and loved the arts. So theatrical, full of charisma and when it came to poetry, the words jumped off the page when Miss Ryan would recite. She would animate every line in a way I will never forget.

I had a truly wonderful Speech and Drama teacher,

Maeve O'Donoghue, growing up and throughout my teenage years in particular she honed and developed my love, knowledge and appreciation for poetry, the language and the power of the voice. It was the extracurricular activity that took me away from the pressures of study and school life. I loved to play with the delivery, the musicality of the vowels and consonants, the rhyme and rhythm, the inflection, the expression in the voice and in the face to engage and tell the story and capture the emotion through this very unique medium.

That passion was solidified further when I went to Trinity College Dublin and began my Bachelor in Acting Studies course at the Samuel Beckett Theatre. Voice Coach Andrea Ainsworth would spend hours dissecting every verse, line, word, syllable and I felt so privileged to have had that time and space to indulge. That was a special time in my life – I was in a bubble, playing, honing, telling, sharing, trying, failing, trying again without the pressure of the industry and the reality of being a jobbing actor!

It wasn't until I taught Speech and Drama myself later on and began to share and explore poetry with my own young students, making new discoveries through their eyes, that I developed a deeper appreciation of the form and discovered how, regardless of the century, certain themes are universal and totally timeless.

And so this poetry anthology feels like the most natural, joyous project I have ever embarked on. I felt like I was back in the dance studio of the Samuel Beckett Theatre 'indulging'! But I want you to indulge with me. I have shared some thoughts on each of the choices but have also left room for yours. Poetry is subjective and open to each individual interpretation, which has always been the beauty of it. The poems reflect big and small moments in the journeys of our lives, from our dreams and our relationships to love and loss, courage and compassion.

I wanted to break down the barrier some might have to poetry; to create an accessible collection of poems you really don't need a degree in English to enjoy. I wanted to encourage a love for this special form. I really wanted to share some of my favourites; the poems that resonated for me at different points in my life and helped to bring comfort. I wanted to share poems that inspire, poems that empathise, poems that encourage us all to pause, but also to persevere. Poems that bring hope for tomorrow...because every day really is a fresh beginning.

The hope and optimism in this poem have helped me through the toughest days. It's a beautiful reminder that this too shall pass, and every day is a new opportunity to begin again.

New Every Morning

Susan Coolidge

Every morn is the world made new.
You who are weary of sorrow and sinning,
Here is a beautiful hope for you, –
A hope for me and a hope for you.

All the past things are past and over;
The tasks are done and the tears are shed.
Yesterday's errors let yesterday cover;
Yesterday's wounds, which smarted and bled,
Are healed with the healing which night has shed.

Yesterday now is a part of forever,
Bound up in a sheaf, which God holds tight,
With glad days, and sad days, and bad days,
    which never
Shall visit us more with their bloom and their blight,
Their fulness of sunshine or sorrowful night.

Let them go, since we cannot re-live them,
Cannot undo and cannot atone;
God in his mercy receive, forgive them!
Only the new days are our own;
To-day is ours, and to-day alone.

Here are the skies all burnished brightly,
Here is the spent earth all re-born,
Here are the tired limbs springing lightly
To face the sun and to share with the morn
In the chrism of dew and the cool of dawn.

Every day is a fresh beginning;
Listen, my soul, to the glad refrain,
And, spite of old sorrow and older sinning,
And puzzles forecasted and possible pain,
Take heart with the day, and begin again.

The resilience of people in the face of adversity never ceases to amaze me. How some people continue to pick themselves up and dust themselves off is incredible. This poem is a reminder of that determination, that innate human ability to start again anew.

Begin

Brendan Kennelly

Begin again to the summoning birds
to the sight of light at the window,
begin to the roar of morning traffic
all along Pembroke Road.
Every beginning is a promise
born in light and dying in dark
determination and exaltation of springtime
flowering the way to work.
Begin to the pageant of queuing girls
the arrogant loneliness of swans in the canal
bridges linking the past and future
old friends passing though with us still.
Begin to the loneliness that cannot end
since it perhaps is what makes us begin,
begin to wonder at unknown faces
at crying birds in the sudden rain
at branches stark in the willing sunlight
at seagulls foraging for bread
at couples sharing a sunny secret
alone together while making good.
Though we live in a world that dreams of ending
that always seems about to give in
something that will not acknowledge conclusion
insists that we forever begin.

I discovered Morgan Harper Nichols's work on social media and she's one of those people who provides the type of content you love to read and reread and share. This poem is one of my favourites from her beautiful book of the same title. It's a reminder that sometimes struggle is necessary for growth and when you are faced with adversity you discover what it is you are truly made of.

All Along You Were Blooming

Morgan Harper Nichols

And the thing about blooming is,
nothing about the process is easy.
It requires every part of you to
stretch upward, with your roots
firmly planted in the ground; and
in the sun; and in the rain, and
wind, you stand anyway, even
against the pull of the soil. And
through it all, one day you will see
all along you were transforming.
This took everything out of you,
but the struggle was beautiful
and necessary for your growth.

I read this poem in peak lockdown, willing and wishing the weeks to pass. Amy's words reframed things in that instant for me – wishing for the future prevents us from appreciating the present. It's a great reminder to live in the moment.

Soon

Amy De Bhrún

Soon.
It'll all be different soon.
It'll all be better soon.
But soon isn't now
And now we are here.
Here we are.
Now.
This moment.
This breath.
It's the only certainty.
Hanging onto soon
Is the noose that will choke you.
Say hello to this moment
And breathe the deepest breath you can.
And soon
Will be the now you were so desperately waiting for.

Busy is often worn as a badge of honour to the detriment of our overall wellbeing. However, this is the type of busy I can absolutely get on board with!

I'm Busy

Brooke Hampton

I'm busy;
but not in the way
most people accept.
I'm busy calming my fear
and finding my courage.
I'm busy listening to my kids.
I'm busy getting in touch
with what is real.
I'm busy growing things and
connecting with the natural world.
I'm busy questioning my answers.
I'm busy being present in my life.

I came across this poem during a staycation in Dingle, Co. Kerry. I can honestly say it made the trip. As soon as I read it, I put the phone down, forgot about work, any reservations I had about taking some time out disappeared and I thoroughly enjoyed the break. It has now become my little holiday mantra.

Leisure

W.H. Davies

What is this life if, full of care,
We have no time to stand and stare?

No time to stand beneath the boughs,
And stare as long as sheep or cows.

No time to see, when woods we pass,
Where squirrels hide their nuts in grass.

No time to see, in broad daylight,
Streams full of stars, like skies at night.

No time to turn at Beauty's glance,
And watch her feet, how they can dance.

No time to wait till her mouth can
Enrich that smile her eyes began.

A poor life this if, full of care,
We have no time to stand and stare.

When I find myself overthinking, anxious or stressed I often turn to Mother Nature, and she generally has the answers. I love this poem for its peace and tranquillity.

The Peace of Wild Things

Wendell Berry

When despair for the world grows in me
and I wake in the night at the least sound
in fear of what my life and my children's lives may be,
I go and lie down where the wood drake
rests in his beauty on the water, and the great
   heron feeds.
I come into the peace of wild things
who do not tax their lives with forethought
of grief. I come into the presence of still water.
And I feel above me the day-blind stars
waiting with their light. For a time
I rest in the grace of the world, and am free.

When I read this poem, for some reason it brought me straight back to my Leaving Cert year, yearning for freedom and an open road. The moment I handed up my final paper, the world suddenly became my oyster!

Freedom

Olive Runner

Give me the long, straight road before me,
    A clear, cold day with a nipping air,
Tall, bare trees to run on beside me,
    A heart that is light and free from care.
Then let me go! – I care not whither
    My feet may lead, for my spirit shall be
Free as the brook that flows to the river,
    Free as the river that flows to the sea.

When I found this poem mid-lockdown, I felt that Francis had read my mind. I went for a solo walk in the woods that day, found a spot where the light was breaking through the branches, stopped and placed my hand on the trunk of a tree and stayed there for a while as a sense of calm came over me. While I always appreciated the healing power of nature, I had never done anything like that before. That day I felt a special connection to Mother Earth, and it was indeed a blessing.

Blessings

Francis Harvey

Yesterday, for some reason I couldn't
understand, I suddenly felt starved of
trees and had to make tracks towards
the beeches of Lough Eske to set my heart
at ease and stand there slowly adjusting
myself to the overwhelming presence of all
those trees. It was like coming back among
people again after living for ages
alone and as I reached out and laid my
right hand in blessing on the trunk of
a beech that had the solidity but not
the coldness of stone I knew it for
the living thing it was under the palm
of my hand as surely as I know the living
sensuousness of flesh and bone and my
blessing was returned a hundredfold
before it was time for me to go home.

We all enter and exit this world the very same way and we have much more in common than we think.

Common Things

Ann Hawkshaw

The sunshine is a glorious thing,
    That comes alike to all;
Lighting the peasant's lowly cot,
    The noble's painted hall.

The moonlight is a gentle thing,
    It through the window gleams
Upon the snowy pillow where
    The happy infant dreams.

It shines upon the fisher's boat
    Out on the lovely sea,
Or where the little lambkins lie
    Beneath the old oak-tree.

The dew-drops on the summer morn
    Sparkle upon the grass;
The village children brush them off
    That through the meadows pass.

There are no gems in monarch's crowns
    More beautiful than they;
And yet we scarcely notice them,
    But tread them off in play.

Poor Robin on the pear-tree sings
  Beside the cottage-door;
The heath-flower fills the air with sweets,
  Upon the pathless moor.

There are as many lovely things,
  As many pleasant tones,
For those who sit by cottage-hearths
  As those who sit on thrones!

This poem was written by the former American First Lady when she was just ten years of age. I taught it to my Speech and Drama students and thought, 'Jackie hit the nail on the head here.' As her husband, John F. Kennedy, later said, 'We are tied to the ocean. And when we go back to the sea, whether it is to sail or to watch it, we are going back from whence we came.'

Sea Joy

Jacqueline Bouvier

When I go down by the sandy shore
I can think of nothing I want more
Than to live by the booming blue sea
As the seagulls flutter round about me

I can run about – when the tide is out
With the wind and the sand and the sea all about
And the seagulls are swirling and diving for fish
Oh – to live by the sea is my only wish.

For the sea swimmers – 'We must have a turn together'. I love that idea of dancing with the ocean. All those good endorphins you get from dancing – the same could be said about the wondrous sea.

You Sea! *from* Song of Myself

Walt Whitman

You sea! I resign myself to you also – I guess what
   you mean,
I behold from the beach your crooked inviting fingers,
I believe you refuse to go back without feeling of me,
We must have a turn together, I undress, hurry me out
   of sight of the land,
Cushion me soft, rock me in billowy drowse,
Dash me with amorous wet, I can repay you.

Sea of stretch'd ground-swells,
Sea breathing broad and convulsive breaths,
Sea of the brine of life and of unshovell'd yet always-
   ready graves,
Howler and scooper of storms, capricious and dainty
   sea,
I am integral with you, I too am of one phase and of
   all phases.

I discovered Anne Casey when compiling this anthology and the discovery was the highlight of this project for me. Her work, in particular her own recitations and introductions online, moved me to tears. Hailing from West Clare, Anne is inspired by her home place and the result is magic.

I will arise and go

(After William Butler Yeats)

Anne Casey

My people are a migrant clan
Prospering not by hook or crook or craft
But by diligent labour and an easy charm
Flung from one small corner
Across every wind-tossed sea
Mountaintop to valley floor
To lay a thousand roadways
Or stand on pavements grey
To explore wild tropical outposts
Hold fast to frozen plains

My people are an itinerant tribe
A heathen spirit tamed
Not by bonds or shackles or shekels
But by music and by elegant words
Though alongside our wanderlust
Cohabits a want in us –
That surges in each nomad breast –
To journey back again, top the last crest
To that first wide view
Across a childhood shore

To feel the heart leap
Like a salmon returned to familial waters
If only – in our dreams

This poem stands out from schooldays. I had a passionate English teacher who delivered it with feeling! I think it's a great reminder of how we all have a responsibility on this earth and an obligation to play our part, particularly in today's world.

'No man is an island'

John Donne

No man is an island,
Entire of itself;
Every man is a piece of the continent,
A part of the main;
If a clod be washed away by the sea,
Europe is the less,
As well as if a promontory were,
As well as if a manor of thy friend's
Or of thine own were;
Any man's death diminishes me,
Because I am involved in mankind;
And therefore never send to know
For whom the bell tolls;
It tolls for thee.

If you have a friend or a friendship like the one depicted here by Sean Brophy, it's safe to say you are very lucky. I read this having not seen my sisters (my best friends) in a long time and I instantly thought of them. I feel so lucky to say every word is true.

Friendship

Sean Brophy

When I think of friends
I think of easy company
Of no masks, ever

I think of shared experience,
That binds together

I think of judgement suspended
I think of understanding
Of walking in each other's shoes

I think of acceptance
Of what we are
I think of belief in what we try to be
In authenticity

I think of you and you and you
My friends,
My dear friends

I think of you.

More recently, when the insecurity of teenage years left us and we set out on our various paths in life, our mom adopted a new title for herself, our 'frank friend without a filter'. She said she would be failing in her duty if she did not deliver the hard truth when required. This one is for her and anyone who tells it like it is!

Friendship

Dinah Maria Mulock Craik

Oh, the comfort – the inexpressible
　　comfort of feeling safe with a person,
　　Having neither to weigh thoughts,
Nor measure words – but pouring them
　　All right out – just as they are –
Chaff and grain together –
　　Certain that a faithful hand will
Take and sift them –
　　Keep what is worth keeping –
And with the breath of kindness
　　Blow the rest away.

I remember watching a Ted Talk with Jane Fonda and she said, 'Women's friendships are a renewable source of power' and how we rarely see that depicted in the media, women loving and caring for one another – I think this poem beautifully depicts the importance of friends old and new.

New Friends and Old Friends

Joseph Parry

Make new friends, but keep the old
Those are silver, these are gold
New-made friendships, like new wine
Age will mellow and refine
Friendships that have stood the test
Of time and change – are surely best
Brow may wrinkle, hair grow gray
Friendship never knows decay
For 'mid old friends, tried and true
Once more we reach and youth renew
But old friends, alas, may die
New friends must their place supply
Cherish friendships in your breast
New is good, but old is best
Make new friends, but keep the old
Those are silver, these are gold

This poem reminds me of the Nicholas Sparks novel and movie The Notebook. Ever the romantic, I count it one of my favourites. Similarly, I think this beautiful poem by Gabriel Fitzmaurice depicts a maturing love, a deep understanding and an ease in one another's company – the comfort of companionship.

Just To Be Beside You Is Enough

Gabriel Fitzmaurice

Just to be beside you is enough,
Just to make your breakfast tea and toast,
To help you with the ware, that kind of stuff,
Just to get the papers and your post;
To hold you in my arms in calm embrace,
Just to sit beside you at the fire,
Just to trace my fingers on your face
Is more to me than all of youth's desire;
Just to lie beside you in the night,
To hear you breathe in peace before I sleep,
To wake beside you in the morning light
In the love we sowed together that we reap.
Together we have taken smooth and rough.
Just to be beside you is enough.

The last two lines of this poem could possibly be my favourite two lines of poetry ever written. The imagery but also the vulnerability in this famous love poem makes it truly endearing.

Aedh Wishes for the Cloths of Heaven

W.B. Yeats

Had I the heavens' embroidered cloths,
Enwrought with golden and silver light,
The blue and the dim and the dark cloths
Of night and light and the half light,
I would spread the cloths under your feet:
But I, being poor, have only my dreams;
I have spread my dreams under your feet;
Tread softly because you tread on my dreams.

Apart from being one of the most beautifully written love sonnets in the English language, I love that Elizabeth Barrett Browning's husband (whom the sonnet is about) was her biggest supporter and champion as a female poet in the nineteenth century, despite her tendency to outshine him in the literary stakes. It makes it all the more romantic.

Sonnet 43

Elizabeth Barrett Browning

How do I love thee? Let me count the ways.
   I love thee to the depth and breadth and height
   My soul can reach, when feeling out of sight
For the ends of Being and ideal Grace.
I love thee to the level of every day's
   Most quiet need, by sun and candlelight.
   I love thee freely, as men strive for Right.
I love thee purely, as they turn from Praise.
I love thee with the passion put to use
   In my old griefs, and with my childhood's faith.
I love thee with a love I seemed to lose
   With my lost saints – I love thee with the breath,
Smiles, tears, of all my life! – and, if God choose,
   I shall but love thee better after death.

It takes courage to fully lean into one's true and authentic self. Own that self-portrait.

Self-Portrait

David Whyte

It doesn't interest me if there is one God
or many gods.
I want to know if you belong or feel
abandoned.
If you know despair or can see it in others.
I want to know
if you are prepared to live in the world
with its harsh need
to change you. If you can look back
with firm eyes
saying this is where I stand. I want to know
if you know
how to melt into that fierce heat of living
falling toward
the center of your longing. I want to know
if you are willing
to live, day by day, with the consequence of love
and the bitter
unwanted passion of your sure defeat.

I have heard in that fierce embrace, even
the gods speak of God.

I had the privilege of reciting this poem at my sister Ailbhe and her husband Ruaidhri's wedding and I have loved it ever since.

Chapter One of One Thousand

O.J. Preston

For two people this dawn brought on a magical day
Now husband and wife they head on their way
As a boat setting sail may their journey begin
With calmest of waters, most helpful of wind
And if they should stumble upon turbulent sea
May it pass them unharming – leave them be.

For here are two people whom love has well bitten
Here opens their book which has yet to be written
As the first page unfolds and their life inks its path
May it write a true story where forever love lasts
Let their journey be happy till death do they part
Of one thousand chapters may this be the start.

This poem stopped me in my tracks. What a beautiful way to describe a relationship that may be past the initial 'honeymoon period'. The last line is my favourite.

A Decade

Amy Lowell

When you came, you were like red wine and honey,
And the taste of you burnt my mouth with its sweetness.
Now you are like morning bread,
Smooth and pleasant.
I hardly taste you at all for I know your savor,
But I am completely nourished.

When loves turns sour – we spent lots of time in college working on Shakespeare's love sonnets but this take on toxic love always interested me. Perhaps for its sheer passion. Of course, there are many beautiful, romantic works to choose from but when things are less than rosy, Sonnet 147!

Sonnet 147

William Shakespeare

My love is as a fever longing still
For that which longer nurseth the disease;
Feeding on that which doth preserve the ill,
The uncertain-sickly appetite to please.
My reason, the physician to my love,
Angry that his prescriptions are not kept,
Hath left me, and I desperate now approve,
Desire is death, which physic did except.
Past cure I am, now reason is past care,
And frantic-mad with evermore unrest:
My thoughts and my discourse as madmen's are,
At random from the truth vainly express'd;
    For I have sworn thee fair, and thought thee bright,
    Who art as black as hell, as dark as night.

It's an immense challenge to single out just one Heaney poem. This one hung in our kitchen at home growing up and always stayed with me – I love the reassuring nature of it. A gorgeous poem for newlyweds, perhaps a couple moving into a new home or anyone at all...

Scaffolding

Seamus Heaney

Masons, when they start upon a building,
Are careful to test out the scaffolding;

Make sure that planks won't slip at busy points,
Secure all ladders, tighten bolted joints.

And yet all this comes down when the job's done
Showing off walls of sure and solid stone.

So if, my dear, there sometimes seem to be
Old bridges breaking between you and me

Never fear. We may let the scaffolds fall
Confident that we have built our wall.

I think this poem by Steve Denehan is one of the most beautiful love poems I have ever read. Of course this is a big statement to make but something about that nostalgia moves me every single time I read it.

A Poem from My Father to My Mother

Steve Denehan

Remember when we met
when I was a kite
when you were the wind
when Dublin was dance-hall days
foggy nights
what-ifs and maybes
remember when I fell into myself
how you forgave me
and forgive me still
remember Burt Bacharach in the hotel lobby
when you exclaimed, 'It's him!'
remember how we used to dance
how the room spun with us
This Guy's in Love with You
remember when you said, 'Yes.'
remember those funhouse mirror years
when you remained a childless mother
remember the worry in your voice
when you threw the word into the air
not knowing if I would catch it
'Adoption...'
remember how I was the fool
who should have held you

more
remember how they grew
in our arms
on our laps
how they left
but never leave
remember when months became decades
and we forgave ourselves
for getting old
remember before
I started
to forget
remember when we ran across the dawn
or wanted to, at least

This is a very personal contribution. As I mentioned in my intro, Dad has been writing poems for us for years. This is a special one he wrote for my husband John and me on our wedding day. I loved it from the moment I read it and felt very proud to recite it that day. Anyone who knows the area of West/North Clare will appreciate the beautiful imagery and deep connection to the landscape. It's always been there for Dad and in turn has been passed on to me.

Doolin Romance

Eugene Garrihy

With my true love we gazed out,
on beauty out of dreams
.Where lunar landscapes kiss the bogs
and gentians speckle greens.

He held my hand on Moher's edge,
Where streams and rivers flow
We watched the puffins break through shells
Revealing coloured glow.

He asked me if I'd be his bride
to love for ever more,
My answer pounding in my heart
You're the one that I adore.

Then gannets dived and salmon leaped
And dolphins danced at sea
A thousand birds of every hue
Sang sweet in harmony.

We tip toed oer those lunar slopes
On this ice created space
With floral carpet at our feet
On the Burren's woven lace.

And music flowed from every house
With roofs of straw and tile.
We danced all night on Moher flags
Then kissed by moonlight stile.

We strolled boreens to heather hills
With scents of mountain thyme
And viewed the church on distant hill
Where now our hands entwine.

A descendent of this place I am,
So someday we might share,
With children and their children too
This jewel in Co Clare.

During the pandemic this poem felt incredibly poign-ant. Human touch is the most natural, innate and comforting thing and all of a sudden it felt so alien. Here's a celebration of it...to remind ourselves.

Holding Hands

Michelle Yeo

At play, for fun
Here are kids just holding hands:
A natural handhold
That says 'I like you;'
Hands creamed with ice cream
Know only fun not stickiness.
In love, in despair,
Here behold the holding of hands:
A tender embrace,
Fingers locked in a twine;
A comforting squeeze of hands
That spells, 'I understand.'
At birth, at death,
Here we witness the holding of hands:
A baby's fingers
Clasping a mother's finger;
A hand all limp and lifeless
Lovingly held to a mourning cheek.
Holding hands is the language of man,
So profound yet simple;
Always touching, infinitely soothing,
Whatever life's precious moment:
At play, for fun
In love, in despair,
At birth, at death,
And all else in between.

'I'll be happy when...'

Perhaps we are all guilty of uttering these words at various stages of our lives. This poem reminds us that we are not defined by physical appearance, material things or indeed anything outside of our true authentic selves. A gentle reminder to always practise self-love and compassion, particularly when you feel the odds may be against you.

Not

Erin Hanson

You are not your age, nor the size of clothes you wear,
You are not a weight, or the color of your hair.
You are not your name, or the dimples in your cheeks.
You are all the books you read, and all the words
    you speak.
You are your croaky morning voice, and the smiles
    you try to hide.
You're the sweetness in your laughter, and every tear
    you've cried.
You're the songs you sing so loudly when you know
    you're all alone.
You're the places that you've been to, and the one
    that you call home.
You're the things that you believe in, and the people
    whom you love.
You're the photos in your bedroom, and the future
    you dream of.
You're made of so much beauty, but it seems that
    you forgot
When you decided that you were defined by all the
    things you're not.

They say the moment a child is born, the parent is also born. That first year is the most transformative year for any new parent. Karen McMillan gives a beautiful raw account of it in this piece, and it brings me instantly back.

That First Year

Karen McMillan

The year that two became three
No. More. Hot. Tea.

The year of not leaving your side
For more than an hour
And feeling revived
From a two minute shower

The year of white noise
Cuddles and baby slings
As you slowly adjust
To the outside things

The year of sleep regressions
Monkey impressions
Panicked Google searches
Too many to mention

The year I realised that women
Really do hold all the powers
Rocking and pacing
For hours and hours

Being more selective of
The company I keep
And dreading that question
So how does he sleep?

The year of building
All the rods for my own back
Binning the baby books
And not looking back

Endless walks with the pram
To help you to nap
Pounding the pavements
Looking like crap

One whole year to realise
That there's no wrong or right
There's what works
What you need
In the middle of the night

The year of doubts and fears
And bending the ears
Of family and friends
He'll sleep eventually
But when?

But you're more than
Your sleep struggles
So much more

You're that look of wonder
At a knock on the door
Your giggles
Your protests
And that tiny roar

Beaming with pride
As you take in your stride
Learning to roll, crawl and stand
And wave your wee hand

A sudden respect for those
Who've done all this before
But with two, with three, with four
Or more

The year of grand plans and dreams
Of these homemade cuisines
But some days just called
For eggs, chips and beans

And yet somehow you thrived
And we just about survived
The hourly wake-ups,
And some almost-breakups

You really did shake-up
These two kids

If poetry wasn't the best medicine, the innocence of a four-year-old surely would be. I have a little girl this very same age so naturally I think this Christopher Morley piece is just magic.

To A Child

Christopher Morley

The greatest poem ever known
Is one all poets have outgrown:
The poetry, innate, untold,
Of being only four years old.

Still young enough to be a part
Of Nature's great impulsive heart,
Born comrade of bird, beast, and tree
And unselfconscious as the bee –

And yet with lovely reason skilled
Each day new paradise to build;
Elate explorer of each sense,
Without dismay, without pretense!

In your unstained transparent eyes
There is no conscience, no surprise:
Life's queer conundrums you accept,
Your strange divinity still kept.

Being, that now absorbs you, all
Harmonious, unit, integral,
Will shred into perplexing bits, –
Oh, contradictions of the wits!

And Life, that sets all things in rhyme,
may make you poet, too, in time —
But there were days, O tender elf,
When you were Poetry itself!

This little Irish poem has a universal message. The days can be long, but the years are short. Cherish them.

Subh Milis

Seamus O Neill

Bhí subh milis
Ar bhaschrann an dorais
Ach mhúch mé an corraí
Ionam a d'éirigh,
Mar smaoinigh mé ar an lá
A bheas an baschrann glan,
Agus an lámh bheag
Ar iarraidh.

Jam

There was jam
On the door handle
But I suppressed the vexation
That rose up in me
Because I thought of the day
That the door handle would be clean
And the little hand
Would be gone.

I often get emotional when reading motherly musings. Maria Tempany documents so many of those moments of overwhelm, sheer joy, vulnerability, guilt, exhaustion and undeniable love so wonderfully. This particular one caught me off guard. It's a little reminder to us all, put the phone away, unplug and simply be.

Mama, Put the Phone Away

Maria Tempany

I got a rude awakening when
My son said to me today
With a look so earnest in his eyes
'Mama, put the phone away'

I was rooted to that very spot
When, yet again, he said
'Mama, put it down, right over there.
Come play with me instead.'

A sense of shame engulfed me.
And all at once I knew
How right he really truly was
Despite his ripe old age of two.

As instructed, down I got,
To play with my sweet boy.
To dissipate that shame I felt,
And replace it with pure joy.

What affirmations we may seek,
Behind these screens we all possess.
Can often be a source of pain,
Upset and much distress.

Did anybody like my post?
A follow? Or a share?
Quite frankly and perhaps he's right
My son really doesn't care.

Of course all these communities
Have an important role to play.
Especially in the times we're in
With those we love at bay.

But for me this simple statement
From the centre of my world.
Struck a cord so painfully
I felt compelled to share this word.

So, one and all, why don't we try
To 'put the phones away'.
Not all the time, just now and then.
And, ever present, try to stay.

There is no denying the beautiful imagery in Emily Brontë's work but I particularly love the final stanza in this piece for the hope and the reference to the sea, to which so many of us turn for solace.

Past, Present, Future

Emily Brontë

Tell me, tell me, smiling child,
What the past is like to thee?
'An Autumn evening soft and mild
With a wind that sighs mournfully.'

Tell me, what is the present hour?
'A green and flowery spray
Where a young bird sits gathering its power
To mount and fly away.'

And what is the future, happy one?
'A sea beneath a cloudless sun;
A mighty, glorious, dazzling sea
Stretching into infinity.'

I have enjoyed this poem with many of my students and it was the first poem I taught my girls. It's an easy poem for the little ones to remember but it also has a big message for us all.

The Little Elf Man

J.K. Bangs

I met a little elf man, once,
   Down where the lilies blow.
I asked him why he was so small,
   And, why he didn't grow.

He slightly frowned, and with his eye
   He looked me through and through.
'I'm just as big for me,' said he,
    'As you are big for you!'

A little farewell poem to our first home.

No. 32

Aoibhín Garrihy

As I lay in this bed for the very last time
Memories of a decade are flooding my mind
And this house that felt big in the early days
Became packed full of love in so many ways.

And before the pitter patter of feet or paws
It was just me and you and all of our flaws
These walls bore witness to some highs and some lows
'If they could speak...' as the saying goes.

We dreamt of this day, a labour of love,
A passion project, a gift from above
But now that it's here, a part of me sighs
Am I ready to leave this huge part of our lives?

A haven, a safe place where our family grew
We danced in the kitchen, we sang in the loo!
The place where suddenly I became we,
Woman turned Mom, two became three...

And now that it's time to say goodbye
There's an air of sadness for those days gone by
Precious times and memories made,
Thank you, house, for all that you gave.

I know it's the natural course of events
But I'll never forget this time that we spent
And if the next abode brings us half the luck
It'll be another great chapter in our life's book.

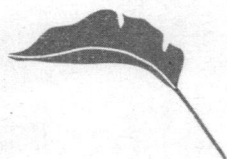

As the poet Denise Blake said herself about this poem, 'sometimes a soft lie is better than the brutal truth'.

And They All Lived Happily

Denise Blake

All the bad guys died in the end.
My kiss did make bruises better.
It was right to put lost teeth under a pillow
and that time, when you didn't find money,
there really was a tooth-fairy holiday.

I told the truth about castor oil
as you have grown big and strong.
Broccoli, porridge, the last bit on your plate,
have been the making of you.
I really believed your Granny would get better.
I didn't think your eyes would possibly stick
that way, but it seemed the thing to say.
That report card wasn't worth all my giving out,
I knew your teacher had a pick against you
but how to admit that to a ten-year-old?

We weren't made of money. I did need a break.
Our dog did go to live on a farm, for a while.
When I said, I'll think about it. I did.
You do know I was right about that girl.
Honestly, most of the time, I told you the truth.

Parenting is the most fulfilling, amazing, rewarding, wondrous job in the world. It is also the most challenging and confusing and deflating at times. We often go to bed at night wondering, 'Should I do more? Can I do better? Where did it go wrong?' With the noise of commercialism bellowing in our ears, this is a little reminder to go easy and keep it simple.

'Do not ask your children to strive'

William Martin

Do not ask your children
to strive for extraordinary lives.
Such striving may seem admirable,
but it is the way of foolishness.
Help them instead to find the wonder
and the marvel of an ordinary life.
Show them the joy of tasting
tomatoes, apples and pears.
Show them how to cry
when pets and people die.
Show them the infinite pleasure
in the touch of a hand.
And make the ordinary come alive for them.
The extraordinary will take care of itself.

Ever felt like the four walls were closing in on you? They say a change is as good as a rest. When I read this poem, I thought of those working/studying/cooking/cleaning/parenting and everything else from home. It can be intense, and the juggle is real! This poem by Edna St. Vincent Millay captures that yearning to make a break for it with an interesting ending too.

Departure

Edna St. Vincent Millay

It's little I care what path I take,
And where it leads it's little I care,
But out of this house, lest my heart break,
I must go, and off somewhere!

It's little I know what's in my heart,
What's in my mind it's little I know,
But there's that in me must up and start,
And it's little I care where my feet go!

I wish I could walk for a day and a night,
And find me at dawn in a desolate place,
With never the rut of a road in sight,
Or the roof of a house, or the eyes of a face.

I wish I could walk till my blood should spout,
And drop me, never to stir again,
On a shore that is wide, for the tide is out,
And the weedy rocks are bare to the rain.

But dump or dock, where the path I take
Brings up, it's little enough I care,
And it's little I'd mind the fuss they'll make,
Huddled dead in a ditch somewhere.

'Is something the matter, dear,' she said,
'That you sit at your work so silently?'
'No, mother, no – 'twas a knot in my thread.
There goes the kettle – I'll make the tea.'

I read this poem on 'one of those days' and needed to read it. Jan Brierton is one of Ireland's most exciting new poets and the final stanza of 'But' is glorious.

But

Jan Brierton

The woman in me is exhausted,
The chef in me is out on strike.
The teacher in me has nothing to teach,
And the mother in me is in strife.

The housekeeper in me is dog tired,
The worker in me is off sick.
The student in me isn't listening,
And the wife in me thinks he's a dick
(Sometimes)

The peacemaker in me can't say sorry,
The friend in me – nothing to give.
The daughter in me pleads 'don't worry'
And the forgetter in me won't forgive.

The supporter in me has no chants left,
The juggler in me dropped the balls.
The reader in me can't finish a book,
And the caller in me dropped the call.

The cleaner in me threw the towel in,
The fashionista in me looks like crap.
The beauty in me, feels more like a beast,
And the gym bunny in me needs a nap.

The talker in me is gone silent,
The carer in me could care less.
The spender in me is insolvent,
And the organiser in me is a mess.

But.

The sharer in me is still sharing,
The thinker in me is still deep.
The lover in me, still has something to give.
And the dreamer in me's not asleep.

Sleep is a fundamental. Something we almost take for granted until we don't get enough of it! I always describe it as the pillar for our overall health and wellbeing and without it we don't eat, move, function properly. Sometimes we crave it so badly we almost beg the universe for it, as Keats does here.

To Sleep

John Keats

O soft embalmer of the still midnight,
　　Shutting, with careful fingers and benign,
Our gloom-pleas'd eyes, embower'd from the light,
　　Enshaded in forgetfulness divine;
O soothest Sleep! if so it please thee, close;
　　In midst of this thine hymn, my willing eyes,
Or wait the amen, ere thy poppy throws
　　Around my bed its lulling charities;
　　Then save me, or the passed day will shine
Upon my pillow, breeding many woes;
　　Save me from curious conscience, that still lords
Its strength for darkness, burrowing like a mole;
　　Turn the key deftly in the oiled wards,
And seal the hushed casket of my soul.

For those who are 'domestically challenged' like myself...this one's for you!

Dust If You Must

Rose Milligan

Dust if you must, but wouldn't it be better
To paint a picture or write a letter,
Bake a cake or plant a seed,
Ponder the difference between want and need?

Dust if you must, but there's not much time,
With rivers to swim and mountains to climb,
Music to hear and books to read,
Friends to cherish and life to lead.

Dust if you must, but the world's out there,
With the sun in your eyes, the wind in your hair,
A flutter of snow, a shower of rain.
This day will not come around again.

Dust if you must, but bear in mind,
Old age will come and it's not kind.
And when you go – and go you must –
You, yourself, will make more dust.

'Love is no less practical than a coffee grinder or a safe spare tire'.

This line should be carved in stone as a reminder to us all. Self-love is the greatest gift you can give yourself.

The Word

Tony Hoagland

Down near the bottom
of the crossed-out list
of things you have to do today,

between 'green thread'
and 'broccoli' you find
that you have penciled 'sunlight.'

Resting on the page, the word
is beautiful, it touches you
as if you had a friend

and sunlight were a present
he had sent you from some place distant
as this morning – to cheer you up,

and to remind you that,
among your duties, pleasure
is a thing,

that also needs accomplishing
Do you remember?
that time and light are kinds

of love, and love
is no less practical
than a coffee grinder

or a safe spare tire?
Tomorrow you may be utterly
without a clue

but today you get a telegram,
from the heart in exile
proclaiming that the kingdom

still exists,
the king and queen alive,
still speaking to their children,

 — to any one among them
who can find the time,
to sit out in the sun and listen.

The pressures of social media and society in general can be crippling. This beautiful piece by Becky Hemsley is a reminder to unplug, detach and give yourself time and space to simply breathe.

Breathe

Becky Hemsley

she sat at the back
and they said she was shy
she led from the front
and they hated her pride

they asked her advice
and then questioned her guidance
they branded her loud
then were shocked by her silence

when she shared no ambition
they said it was sad
so she told them her dreams
and they said she was mad

they told her they'd listen
then covered their ears
and gave her a hug
whilst they laughed at her fears

and she listened to all of it
thinking she should
be the girl they told her to be
best as she could

but one day she asked
what was best for herself
instead of trying
to please everyone else

so she walked to the forest
and stood with the trees
she heard the wind whisper
and dance with the leaves

and she spoke to the willow,
the elm and the pine
and she told them what she'd been told
time after time

she told them she never
felt nearly enough
she was either too little
or far, far too much

too loud or too quiet
too fierce or too weak
too wise or too foolish
too bold or too meek

then she found a small clearing
surrounded by firs
and she stopped and she heard
what the trees said to her

and she sat there for hours
not wanting to leave
for the forest said nothing...
it just let her breathe

For Mom.

My Mother

Ann Taylor

Who fed me from her gentle breast,
And hushed me in her arms to rest,
And on my cheek sweet kisses prest?
                    My Mother.

When sleep forsook my open eye,
Who was it sung sweet lullaby,
And rocked me that I should not cry?
                    My Mother.

Who sat and watched my infant head,
When sleeping in my cradle bed,
And tears of sweet affection shed?
                    My Mother.

When pain and sickness made me cry,
Who gazed upon my heavy eye,
And wept for fear that I should die?
                    My Mother.

Who ran to help me when I fell,
And would some pretty story tell,
Or kiss the part to make it well?
                    My Mother.

Who taught my infant lips to pray,
To love God's holy word and day,
And walk in wisdom's pleasant way?
                    My Mother.

And can I ever cease to be
Affectionate and kind to thee,
Who was so very kind to me?
                    My Mother.

Oh, no! the thought I cannot bear,
And, if God please my life to spare,
I hope I shall reward thy care,
                    My Mother.

When thou art feeble, old and grey,
My healthy arm shall be thy stay,
And I will soothe thy pains away,
                    My Mother.

And when I see thee hang thy head,
'Twill be my turn to watch thy bed,
And tears of sweet affection shed,
                    My Mother.

I read this poem the night before a work trip abroad and it resonated so strongly with me. The level of planning involved to simply get out the door when you have smallies is no joke! I had all meals prepped, outfits laid out, instructions written and on the fridge, and of course I knew they were in safe hands yet STILL felt guilty leaving. This poem seemed to articulate those feelings.

Any Woman

Katharine Tynan

I am the pillars of the house;
The keystone of the arch am I.
Take me away, and roof and wall
Would fall to ruin me utterly.

I am the fire upon the hearth,
I am the light of the good sun,
I am the heat that warms the earth,
Which else were colder than a stone.

At me the children warm their hands;
I am their light of love alive.
Without me cold the hearthstone stands,
Nor could the precious children thrive.

I am the twist that holds together
The children in its sacred ring,
Their knot of love, from whose close tether
No lost child goes a-wandering.

I am the house from floor to roof,
I deck the walls, the board I spread;
I spin the curtains, warp and woof,
And shake the down to be their bed.

I am their wall against all danger,
Their door against the wind and snow,
Thou Whom a woman laid in a manger,
Take me not till the children grow!

After loss, we often feel guilt. This is a beautiful poem encouraging the mourner to begin to smile and live again.

Remember Me

Christina Rossetti

Remember me when I am gone away,
Gone far away into the silent land;
When you can no more hold me by the hand,
Nor I half turn to go, yet turning stay.
Remember me when no more day by day
You tell me of our future that you planned:
Only remember me; you understand
It will be late to counsel then or pray.
Yet if you should forget me for a while
And afterwards remember, do not grieve:
For if the darkness and corruption leave
A vestige of the thoughts that once I had,
Better by far you should forget and smile
Than that you should remember and be sad.

For my grandad, Chris Droney.

Grandad

Aoibhín Garrihy

I see you in us all
The best part of us all
The part of us that sees the good
Takes pride and stands up tall

The part of us that never settles
The part that does things right
The part of us up for the craic
That will dance and laugh all night

The part of us that listens
Loves stories and a chat
The part that worries, gives advice
And dons the carer's hat

The part that loves the simple things
But loves the nice things too
Sucky sweets, the motor car,
A well-kept lawn, a polished shoe

The part of us that lives for music
And all the joy it brings
The part that loves the get-together
As we tap along and sing

The part of us that loves family
The part that loves our home
The part that loves our place, our country
To travel and to roam

I see you in my Mom
My sisters and in me
I pray I'll see you in my girls
How lucky would they be?

So when we pause to think of you
Or they talk of your legacy
I'll only have to look around
You've passed it on, you see

For those missing a loved one…

Perhaps

Vera Brittain

Perhaps some day the sun will shine again,
    And I shall see that still the skies are blue,
And feel once more I do not live in vain,
    Although bereft of You.

Perhaps the golden meadows at my feet
    Will make the sunny hours of Spring seem gay,
And I shall find the white May blossoms sweet,
    Though You have passed away.

Perhaps the summer woods will shimmer bright,
    And crimson roses once again be fair,
And autumn harvest fields a rich delight,
    Although You are not there.

Perhaps some day I shall not shrink in pain
    To see the passing of the dying year,
And listen to the Christmas songs again,
    Although You cannot hear.

But, though kind Time may many joys renew,
    There is one greatest joy I shall not know
Again, because my heart for loss of You
    Was broken, long ago.

A 'glass half full' poem if ever needed. I just love Brontë's hope and optimism throughout this piece.

Life

Charlotte Brontë

Life, believe, is not a dream
    So dark as sages say;
Oft a little morning rain
    Foretells a pleasant day.
Sometimes there are clouds of gloom,
    But these are transient all;
If the shower will make the roses bloom,
    Oh, why lament its fall?
        Rapidly, merrily,
    Life's sunny hours flit by,
        Gratefully, cheerily,
    Enjoy them as they fly!

What though Death at times steps in,
    And calls our best away?
What though sorrow seems to win,
    O'er hope, a heavy sway?
Yet Hope again elastic springs,
    Unconquered, though she fell;
Still buoyant are her golden wings,
    Still strong to bear us well.
        Manfully, fearlessly,
    The day of trial bear,
        For gloriously, victoriously,
    Can courage quell despair!

I loved this poem even before knowing Amelia Earhart's story. She was the first woman to fly solo across the Atlantic Ocean, in 1932.

Courage

Amelia Earhart

Courage is the price that Life exacts for granting
    peace.

The soul that knows it not knows no release
From little things:

Knows not the livid loneliness of fear,
Nor mountain heights where bitter joy can hear
The sound of wings.

How can life grant us boon of living, compensate
For dull gray ugliness and pregnant hate
Unless we dare

The soul's dominion? Each time we make a choice,
    we pay
With courage to behold the resistless day,
And count it fair.

No good deed or act of kindness, however small, is ever in vain.

If I Can Stop One Heart from Breaking

Emily Dickinson

If I can stop one heart
from breaking,
I shall not live in vain;

If I can ease one life the aching,
Or cool one pain,

Or help one fainting robin
Unto his nest again,

I shall not live in vain.

In an age of anxiety, insomnia, stress...how wonderful to end the day utterly fulfilled and totally content.

Happy the Man

John Dryden

Happy the man, and happy he alone,
    He who can call today his own:
    He who, secure within, can say,
Tomorrow do thy worst, for I have lived today.
    Be fair or foul or rain or shine
The joys I have possessed, in spite of fate, are mine.
Not Heaven itself upon the past has power,
But what has been, has been, and I have had my hour.

It's OK not to be OK...a beautiful poem about self-compassion.

The Mountain

Laura Ding-Edwards

If the mountain seems too big today
then climb a hill instead.
If the morning brings you sadness
it's ok to stay in bed.
If the day ahead weighs heavy
and your plans feel like a curse,
there's no shame in rearranging,
don't make yourself feel worse.
If a shower stings like needles
and a bath feels like you'll drown,
if you haven't washed your hair for days,
don't throw away your crown.
A day is not a lifetime
a rest is not defeat,
don't think of it as failure,
just a quiet, kind retreat.
It's ok to take a moment
from an anxious, fractured mind,
the world will not stop turning
while you get realigned.
The mountain will still be there
when you want to try again,
you can climb it in your own time,
just love yourself til then.

Dating back to the 1800s, there are lines from this poem that will be familiar to many. It's a reminder of our innate ability to dream, to believe and to achieve.

From **The Music-Makers**

Arthur O'Shaughnessy

We are the music-makers,
    And we are the dreamers of dreams,
Wandering by lone sea-breakers,
    And sitting by desolate streams;
World-losers and world-forsakers,
    On whom the pale moon gleams;
Yet we are the movers and shakers
    Of the world for ever, it seems.

With wonderful deathless ditties
We build up the world's great cities,
    And out of a fabulous story
    We fashion an empire's glory:
One man with a dream, at pleasure,
    Shall go forth and conquer a crown;
And three with a new song's measure
    Can trample an empire down.

We, in the ages lying
    In the buried past of the earth,
Built Ninevah with our sighing,
    And Babel itself with our mirth;
And o'erthrew them with prophesying
    To the old of the new world's worth;
For each age is a dream that is dying,
    Or one that is coming to birth.

Kindness matters.

Count That Day Lost

George Eliot

If you sit down at set of sun
And count the acts that you have done,
And, counting, find
One self-denying deed, one word
That eased the heart of him who heard,
One glance most kind
That fell like sunshine where it went –
Then you may count that day well spent.

But if, through all the livelong day,
You've cheered no heart, by yea or nay –
If, through it all
You've nothing done that you can trace
That brought the sunshine to one face –
No act most small
That helped some soul and nothing cost –
Then count that day as worse than lost.

This is one I remember fondly from schooldays. I loved it even as a teenager. I've always been a bit of a risk-taker so taking the road 'less travelled by' has always appealed to me. I think it's a lovely reminder to weigh things up beforehand but ultimately, go with your gut instinct. It generally serves us well.

The Road Not Taken

Robert Frost

Two roads diverged in a yellow wood,
And sorry I could not travel both
And be one traveler, long I stood
And looked down one as far as I could
To where it bent in the undergrowth;

Then took the other, as just as fair,
And having perhaps the better claim,
Because it was grassy and wanted wear;
Though as for that the passing there
Had worn them really about the same,

And both that morning equally lay
In leaves no step had trodden black.
Oh, I kept the first for another day!
Yet knowing how way leads on to way,
I doubted if I should ever come back.

I shall be telling this with a sigh
Somewhere ages and ages hence:
Two roads diverged in a wood, and I —
I took the one less traveled by,
And that has made all the difference.

Positive self-talk can be a game changer so here's a little reminder to ignore (or take with a pinch of salt) the voice of your inner critic.

Thinking

Walter D. Wintle

If you think you are beaten, you are;
    If you think you dare not, you don't.
If you'd like to win, but think you can't,
    It is almost a cinch you won't.

If you think you'll lose, you're lost,
    For out in the world we find
Success begins with a fellow's will —
    It's all in the state of mind.

If you think you're outclassed, you are;
    You've got to think high to rise;
You've got to be sure of yourself before
    You can ever win a prize.

Life's battles don't always go
    To the stronger or faster man;
But soon or late the man who wins,
    Is the man who thinks he can.

A hugely popular and inspirational poem. Dating back to the 1800s, 'If' continues to win the hearts of many.

If –

Rudyard Kipling

If you can keep your head when all about you
    Are losing theirs and blaming it on you;
If you can trust yourself when all men doubt you,
    But make allowance for their doubting too;
If you can wait and not be tired by waiting,
    Or being lied about, don't deal in lies,
Or being hated, don't give way to hating,
    And yet don't look too good, nor talk too wise;

If you can dream – and not make dreams your master;
    If you can think – and not make thoughts your aim,
If you can meet with Triumph and Disaster
    And treat those two impostors just the same;
If you can bear to hear the truth you've spoken
    Twisted by knaves to make a trap for fools,
Or watch the things you gave your life to, broken,
    And stoop and build 'em up with worn-out tools;

If you can make one heap of all your winnings
    And risk it on one turn of pitch-and-toss,
And lose, and start again at your beginnings
    And never breathe a word about your loss;
If you can force your heart and nerve and sinew
    To serve your turn long after they are gone,
And so hold on when there is nothing in you
    Except the Will which says to them: 'Hold on!'

If you can talk with crowds and keep your virtue,
    Or walk with Kings – nor lose the common touch,
If neither foes nor loving friends can hurt you,
    If all men count with you, but none too much;
If you can fill the unforgiving minute
    With sixty seconds' worth of distance run,
Yours is the Earth and everything that's in it,
    And – which is more – you'll be a Man, my son!

I think this is the ultimate mirror 'pep talk'. When the chips are down, we discover what it is we are truly made of. I believe it was one of Nelson Mandela's favourites too and he recited it on Robben Island.

Invictus

W.E. Henley

Out of the night that covers me,
    Black as the pit from pole to pole,
I thank whatever gods may be
    For my unconquerable soul.

In the fell clutch of circumstance
    I have not winced nor cried aloud.
Under the bludgeonings of chance
    My head is bloody, but unbowed.

Beyond this place of wrath and tears
    Looms but the Horror of the shade,
And yet the menace of the years
    Finds and shall find me unafraid.

It matters not how strait the gate,
    How charged with punishments the scroll,
I am the master of my fate,
    I am the captain of my soul.

For anyone prepared to lift their head above the parapet, who has the courage to step into the ring, whatever form that takes, this piece is for you (and remember, it's easy to comment from the sidelines!).

The Man in the Arena

Theodore Roosevelt

It is not the critic who counts; not the man who
points out how the strong man stumbles, or where
the doer of deeds could have done them better.

The credit belongs to the man who is actually
in the arena, whose face is marred by dust and sweat
and blood; who strives valiantly; who errs, who comes
short again and again, because there is no effort
without error and shortcoming; but who does actually
strive to do the deeds; who knows great enthusiasms,
the great devotions; who spends himself in a worthy
cause; who at the best knows in the end the triumph
of high achievement, and who at the worst, if he
fails, at least fails while daring greatly, so that his
place shall never be with those cold and timid
souls who neither know victory nor defeat.

My mom would often say, 'It's nice to be important but it's far more important to be nice.' This is a wonderful reminder that we are all simply 'passing through' and so, adopting a humble approach is the way to go. The simplicity of the analogy is what I really love about this poem.

Indispensable Man

Saxon White Kessinger

Sometime when you're feeling important;
Sometime when your ego's in bloom
Sometime when you take it for granted
You're the best qualified in the room,

Sometime when you feel that your going
Would leave an unfillable hole,
Just follow these simple instructions
And see how they humble your soul;

Take a bucket and fill it with water,
Put your hand in it up to the wrist,
Pull it out and the hole that's remaining
Is a measure of how you'll be missed.

You can splash all you wish when you enter,
You may stir up the water galore,
But stop and you'll find that in no time
It looks quite the same as before.

The moral of this quaint example
Is do just the best that you can,
Be proud of yourself but remember,
There's no indispensable man.

A firm favourite of my mom's – 'Desiderata'. It's packed with real gems to live by and each time you read it a new line will jump out and resonate. It's a great one to revisit time and time again.

Desiderata

Max Ehrmann

Go placidly amid the noise and the haste, and remember what peace there may be in silence. As far as possible, without surrender, be on good terms with all persons.

Speak your truth quietly and clearly; and listen to others, even to the dull and the ignorant; they too have their story.

Avoid loud and aggressive persons; they are vexatious to the spirit. If you compare yourself with others, you may become vain or bitter, for always there will be greater and lesser persons than yourself.

Enjoy your achievements as well as your plans. Keep interested in your own career, however humble; it is a real possession in the changing fortunes of time.

Exercise caution in your business affairs, for the world is full of trickery. But let this not blind you to what virtue there is; many persons strive for high ideals, and everywhere life is full of heroism.

Be yourself. Especially, do not feign affection. Neither be cynical about love; for in the face of all aridity and disenchantment, it is as perennial as the grass.

Take kindly the counsel of the years, gracefully surrendering the things of youth.

Nurture strength of spirit to shield you in sudden misfortune. But do not distress yourself with dark imaginings. Many fears are born of fatigue and loneliness.

Beyond a wholesome discipline, be gentle with yourself. You are a child of the universe no less than the trees and the stars; you have a right to be here.

And whether or not it is clear to you, no doubt the universe is unfolding as it should. Therefore be at peace with God, whatever you conceive Him to be. And whatever your labors and aspirations, in the noisy confusion of life, keep peace in your soul. With all its sham, drudgery and broken dreams, it is still a beautiful world. Be cheerful. Strive to be happy.

The title of this poem is a mantra for life. Everything is temporary.

This, Too, Shall Pass Away

Lanta Wilson Smith

When some great sorrow, like a mighty river,
Flows through your life with peace-destroying power,
And dearest things are swept from sight forever,
Say to your heart each trying hour:
'This, too, shall pass away.'

When ceaseless toil has hushed your song of
   gladness,
And you have grown almost too tired to pray,
Let this truth banish from your heart its sadness,
And ease the burdens of each trying day:
'This, too, shall pass away.'

When fortune smiles, and, full of mirth and pleasure,
The days are flitting by without a care,
Lest you should rest with only earthly treasure,
Let these few words their fullest import bear:
'This, too, shall pass away.'

When earnest labor brings you fame and glory,
And all earth's noblest ones upon you smile,
Remember that life's longest, grandest story
Fills but a moment in earth's little while:
'This, too, shall pass away.'

Our natural instinct is to fight what we fear but often when we reframe our mindset and arrive at a place of acceptance it can make all the difference.

Allow

Danna Faulds

There is no controlling life.
Try corralling a lightning bolt,
containing a tornado. Dam a
stream, and it will create a new
channel. Resist, and the tide
will sweep you off your feet.
Allow, and grace will carry
you to higher ground. The only
safety lies in letting it all in –
the wild with the weak; fear,
fantasies, failures and success.
When loss rips off the doors of
the heart, or sadness veils your
vision with despair, practice
becomes simply bearing the truth.
In the choice to let go of your
known way of being, the whole
world is revealed to your new eyes.

This reminds me of one of my favourite quotes by Erin Hanson, 'And you ask, what if I fall? Oh but my darling, what if you fly?'

That risk is worth taking. If you never try, you'll never know.

Come to the Edge

Christopher Logue

Come to the edge.
We might fall.
Come to the edge.
It's too high!
COME TO THE EDGE!
And they came,
And he pushed,
And they flew.

Index of First Lines

Acknowledgements

The editor and publisher gratefully acknowledge permission to reproduce the following copyright poems in this book:

Wendell Berry: Wendell Berry, 'The Peace of Wild Things' from *New Collected Poems*. Copyright © 2012 by Wendell Berry. Reprinted with the permission of The Permissions Company, LLC on behalf of Counterpoint Press, counterpointpress.com.

Denise Blake: 'And They All Lived Happily' by Denise Blake from 'Invocation', Revival Press – Limerick Writers Centre © 2018.

Jan Brierton: 'But' a new poem by Jan Brierton © 2022 reproduced by kind permission of Jan Brierton.

Vera Brittain: Vera Brittain's 'Perhaps' is reproduced by permission of Mark Bostridge and T.J. Brittain-Catlin, Literary Executors for the Estate of Vera Brittain 1970.

Sean Brophy: 'Friendship' by Sean Brophy from *The Awakening and Other Poems*, Rainsford Press, 1992.

About the Author

Aoibhín Garrihy is an actress, voiceover artist, entrepreneur and social media influencer. Having graduated with a BA in Acting Studies at Trinity College Dublin in 2009, she became well known for her work in TV dramas such as *Fair City*, *The Fall* and on stage productions at The Gate Theatre. In recent years she co-founded renowned lifestyle and wellness brand BEO. She lives in Co Clare with her husband John and three young daughters.